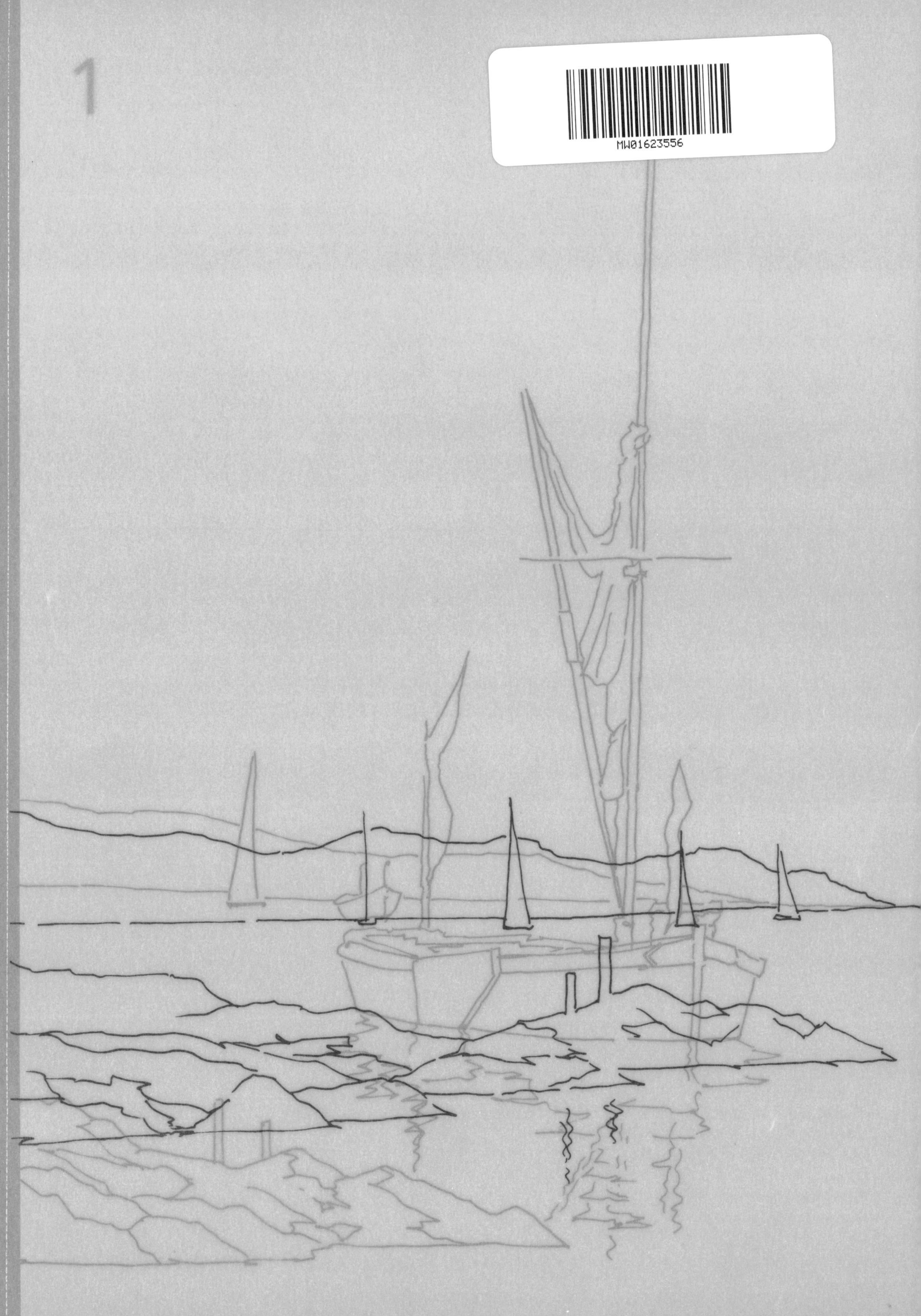
1
MW01623556

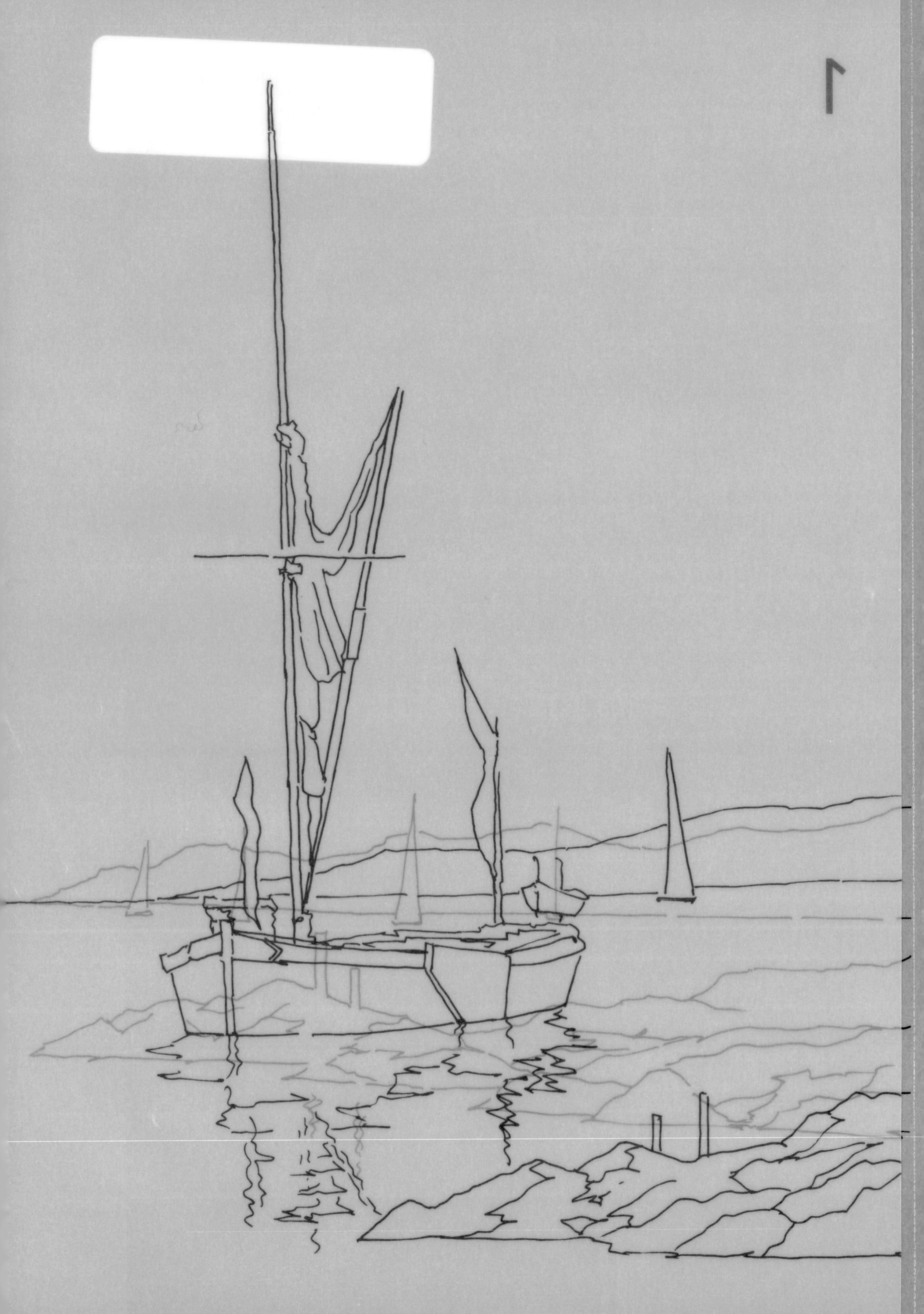

2

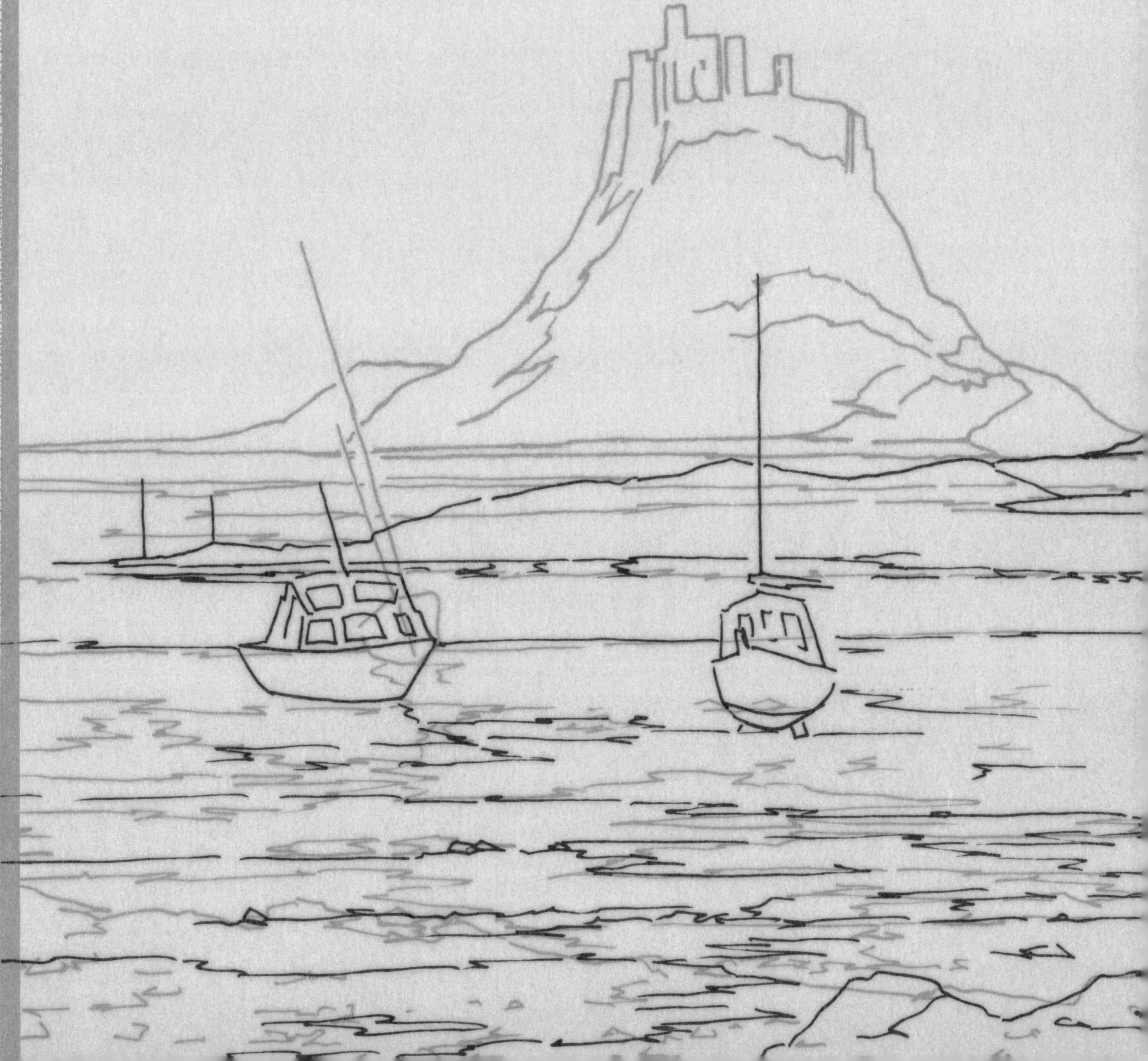

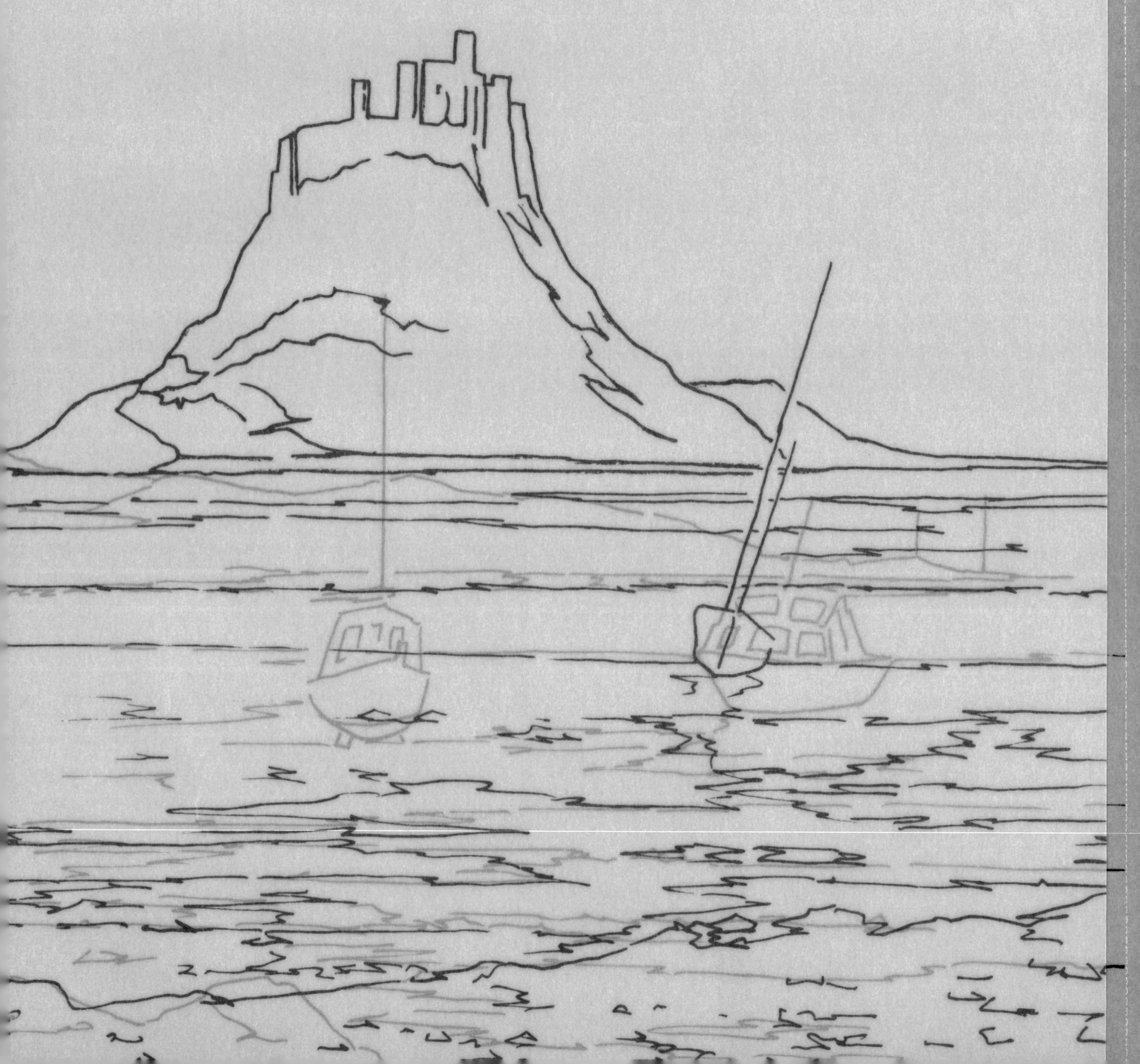

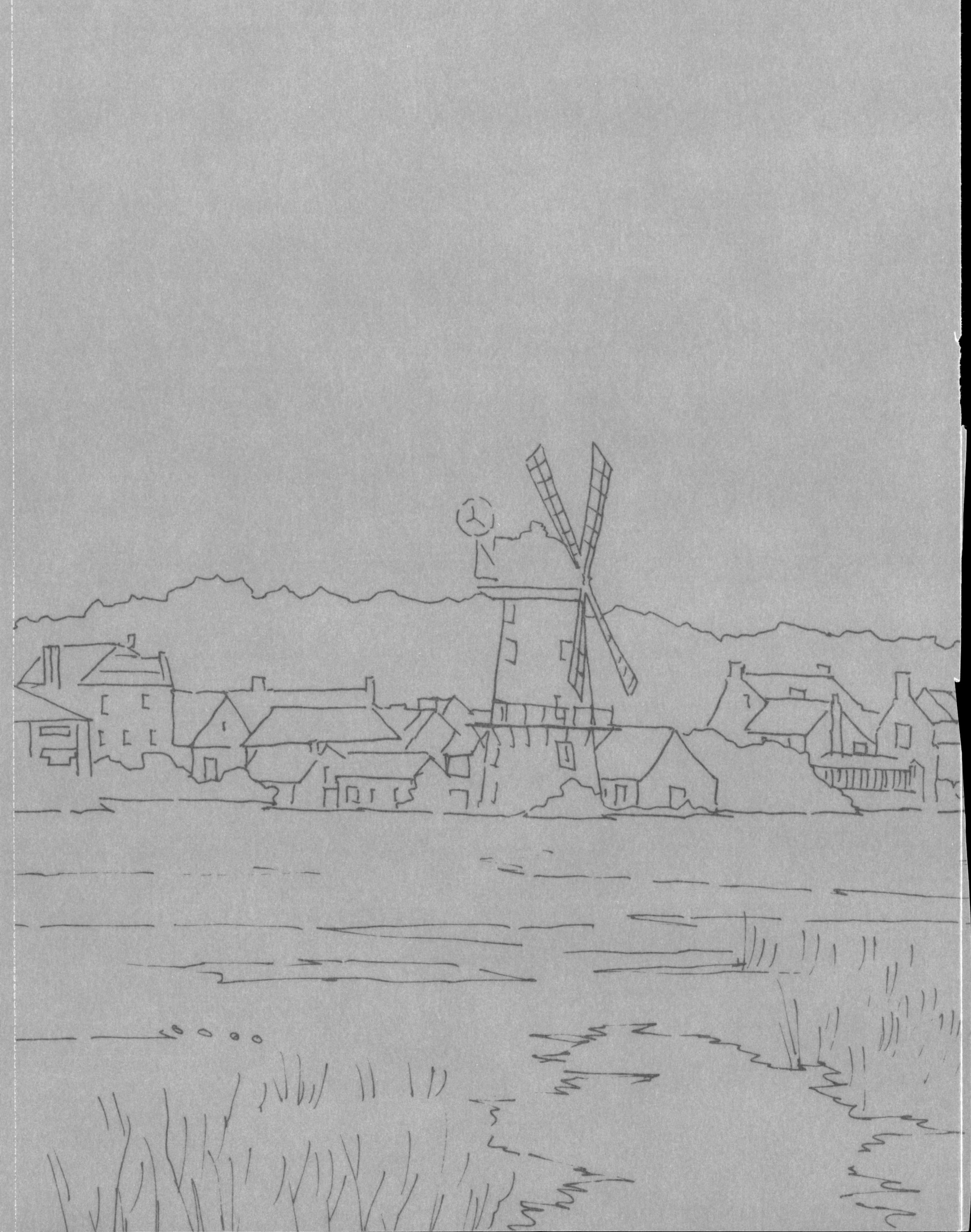

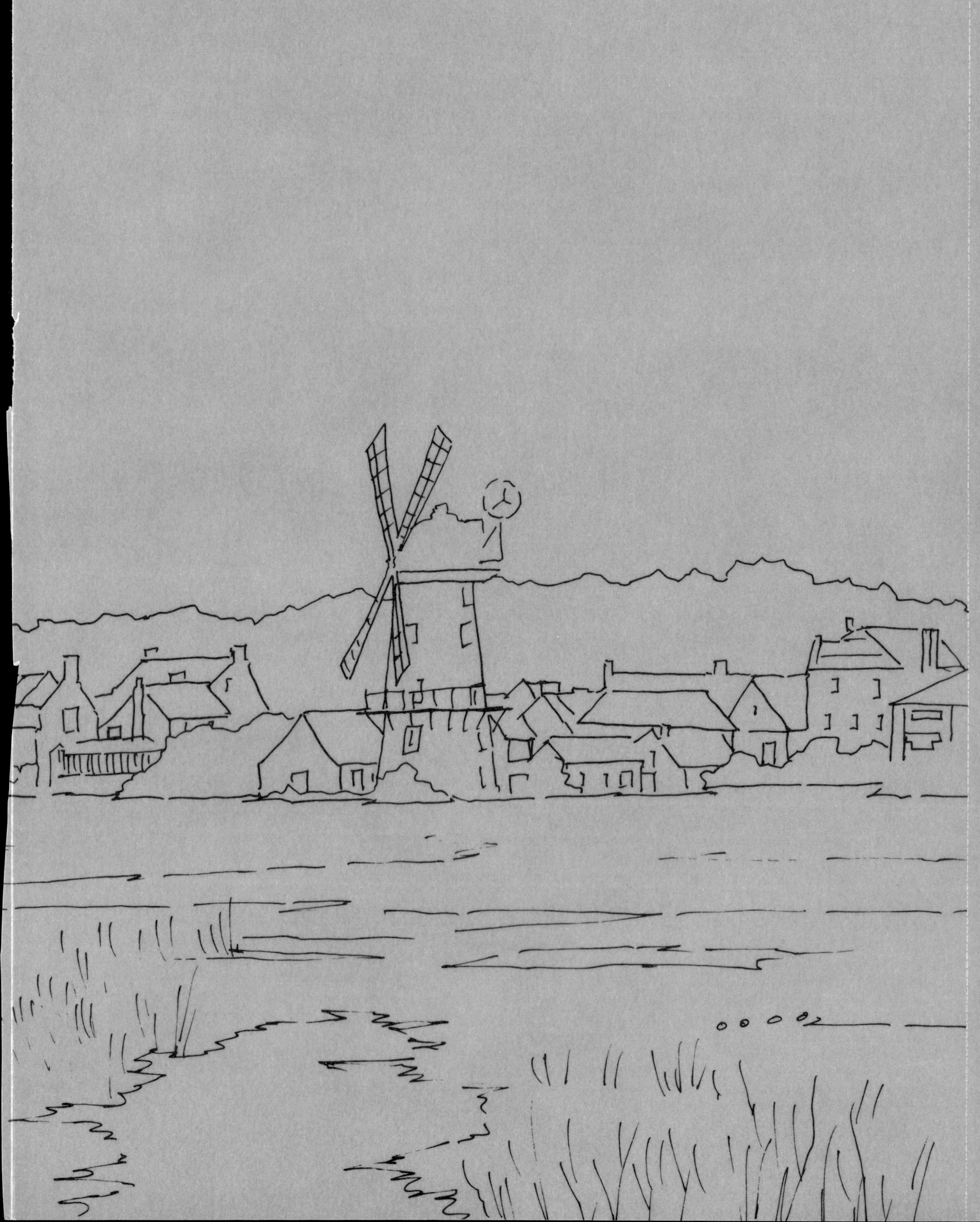

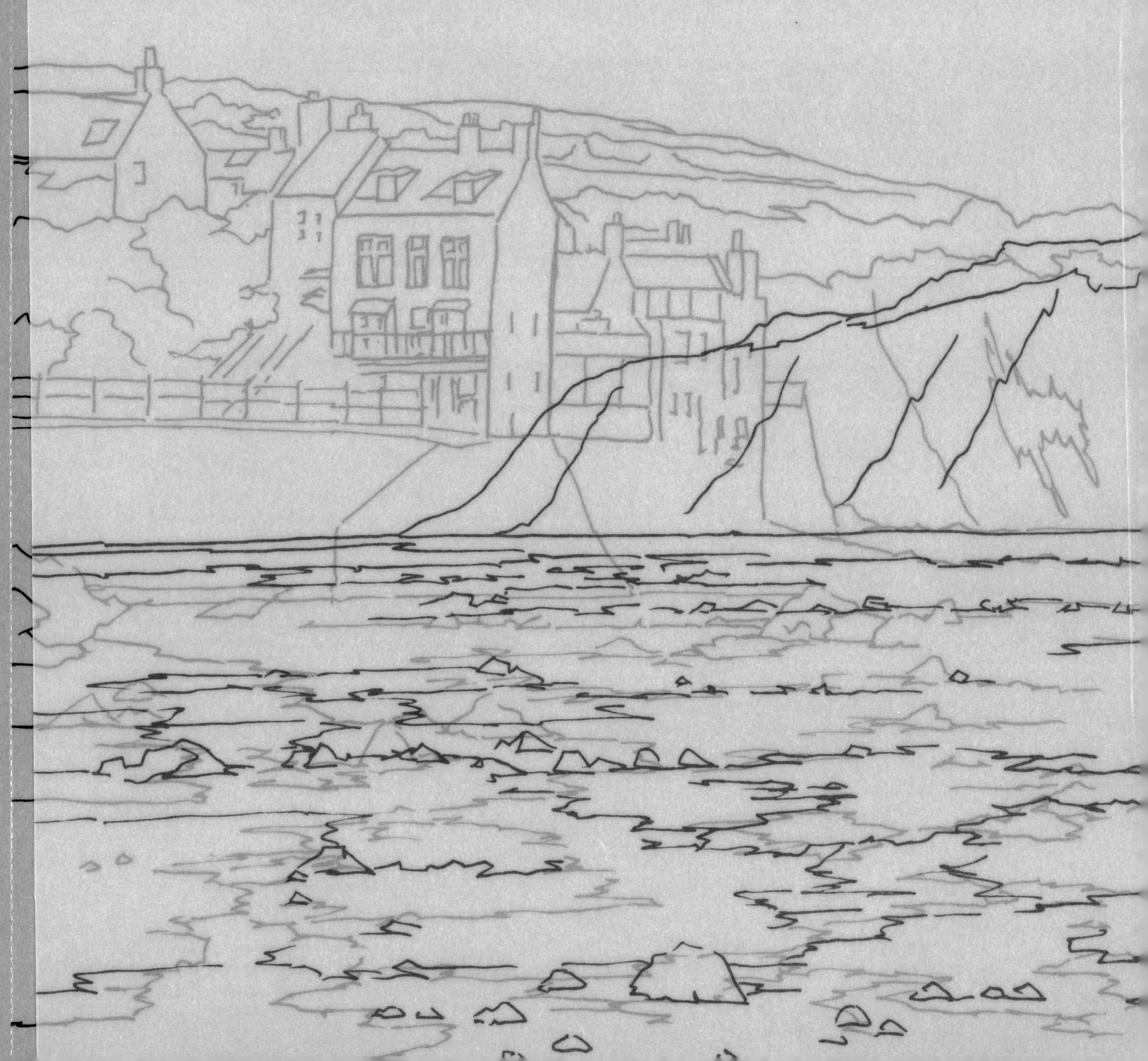

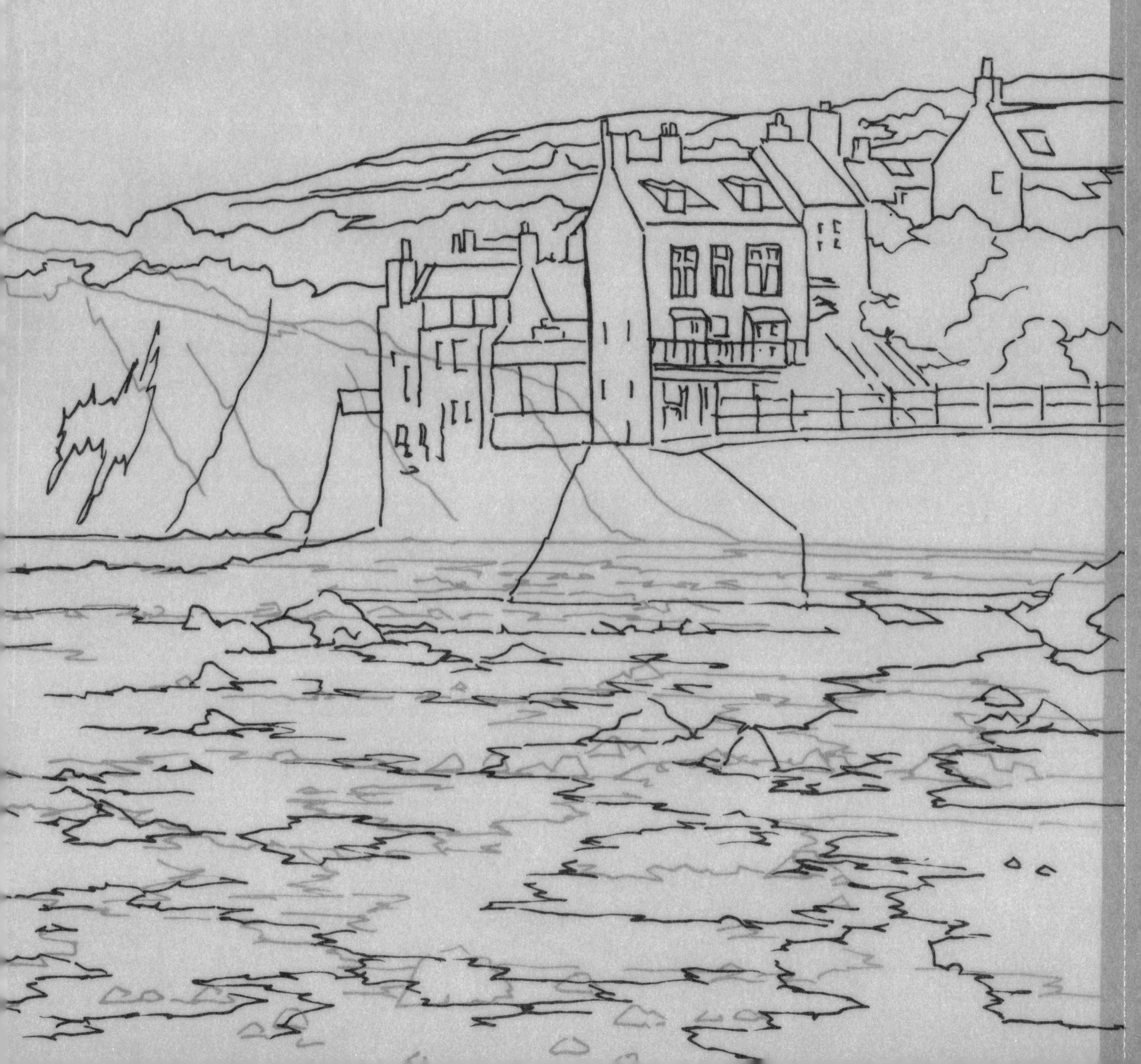

5

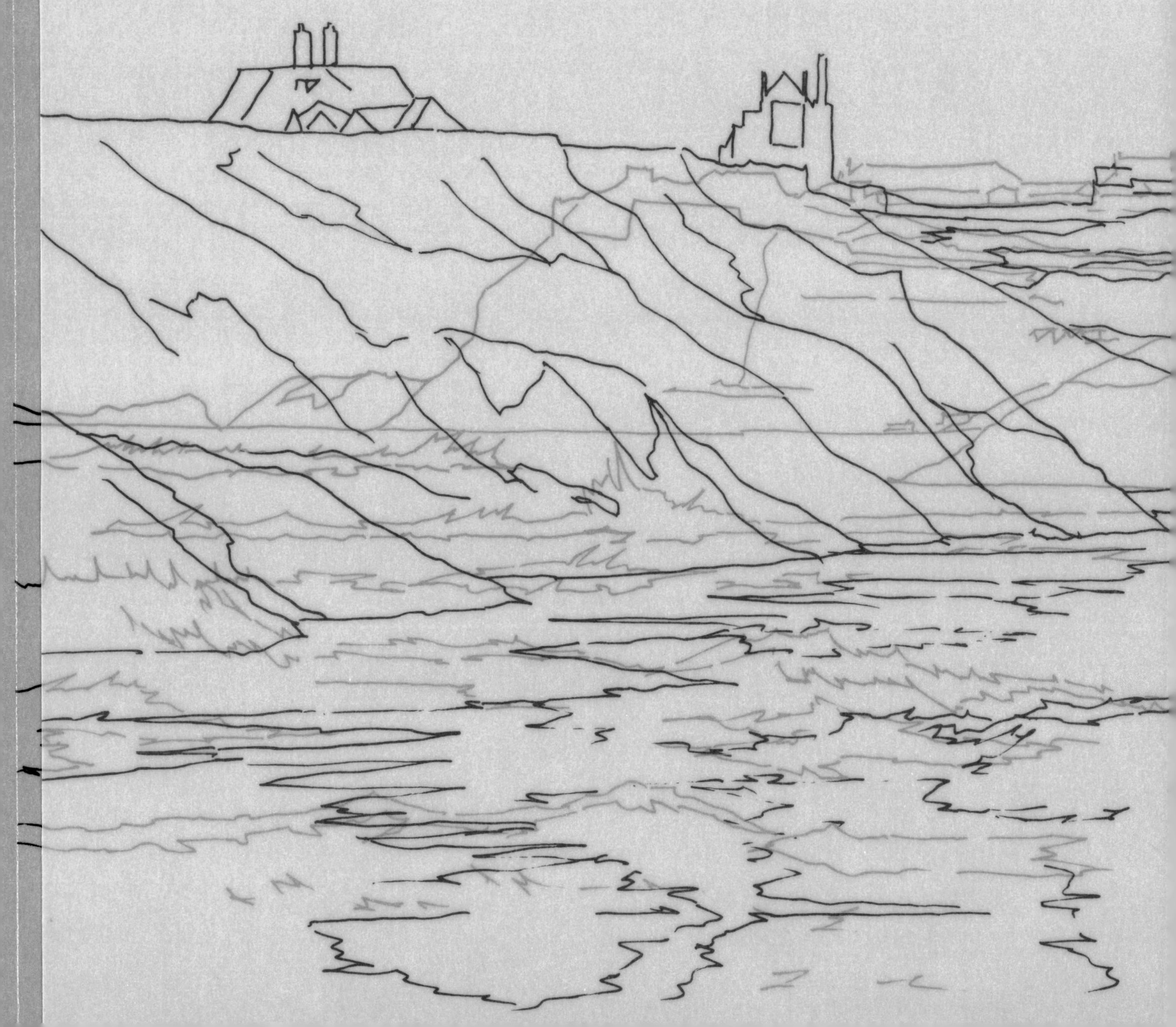

5

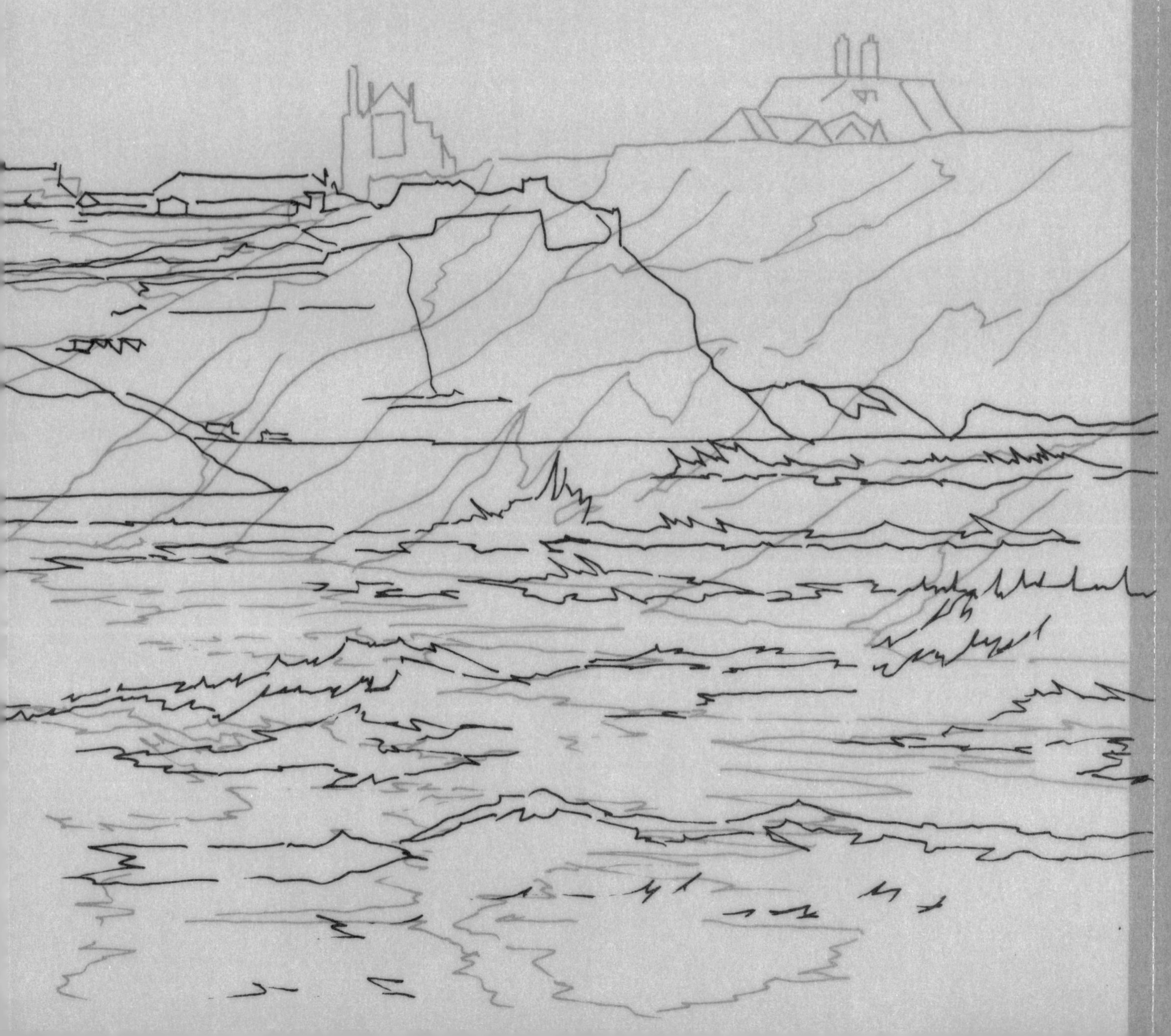

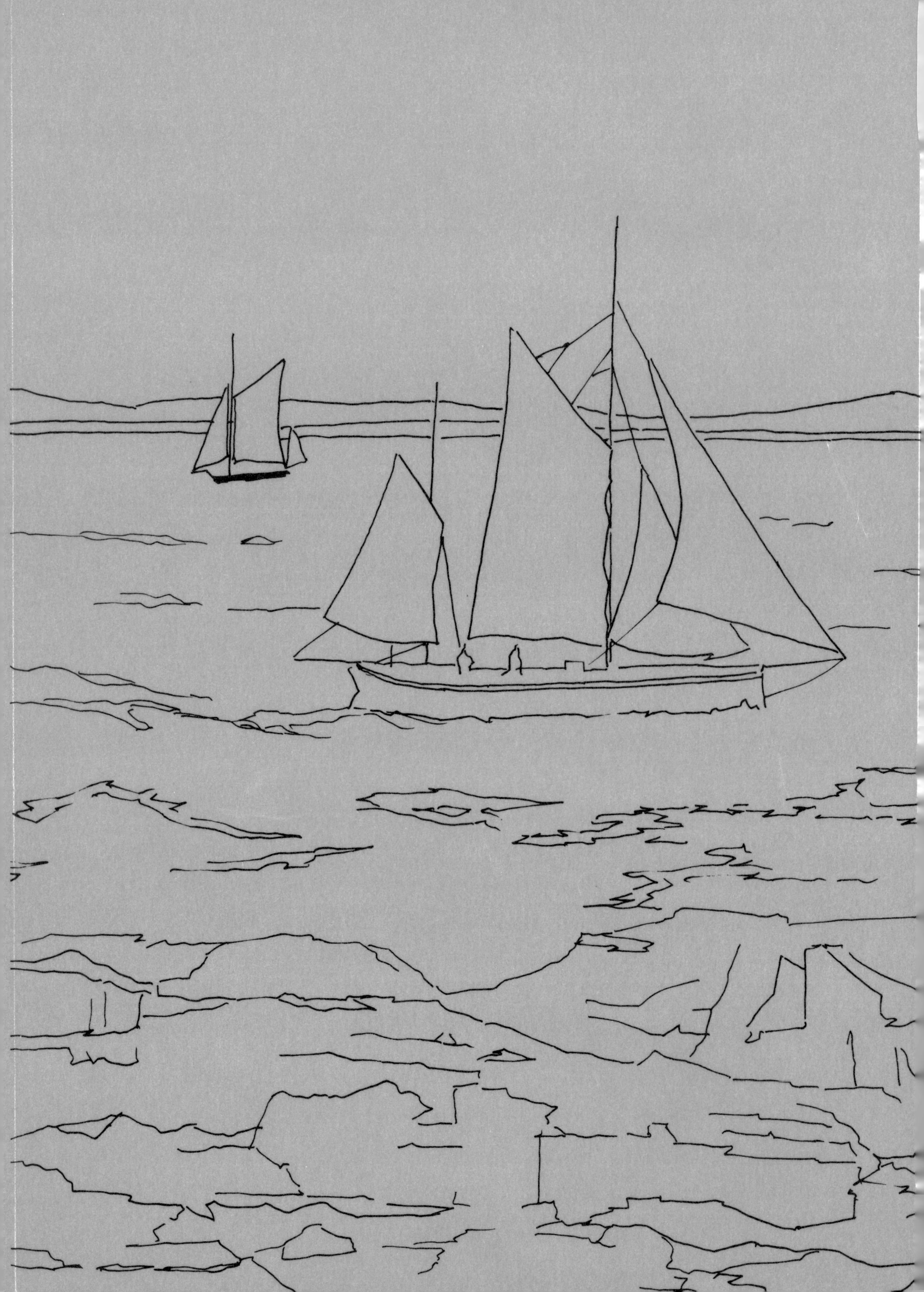

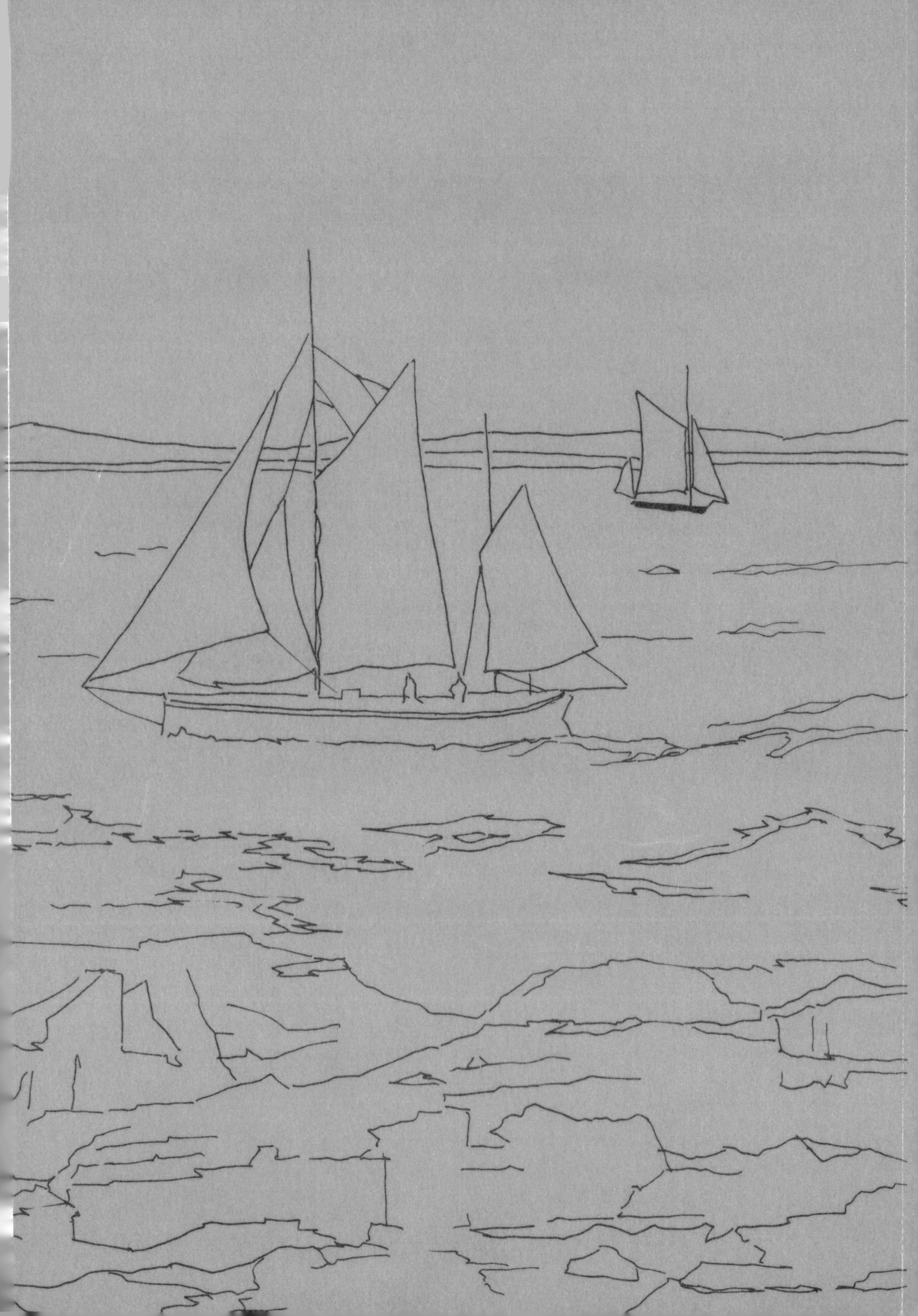

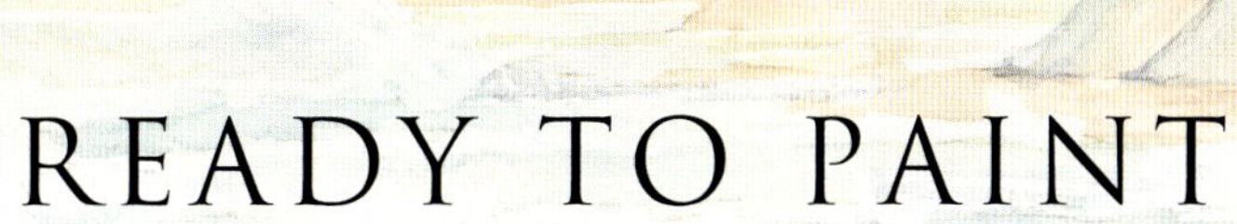
READY TO PAINT

Coastal Landscapes
in Watercolour

Tony Cowlishaw

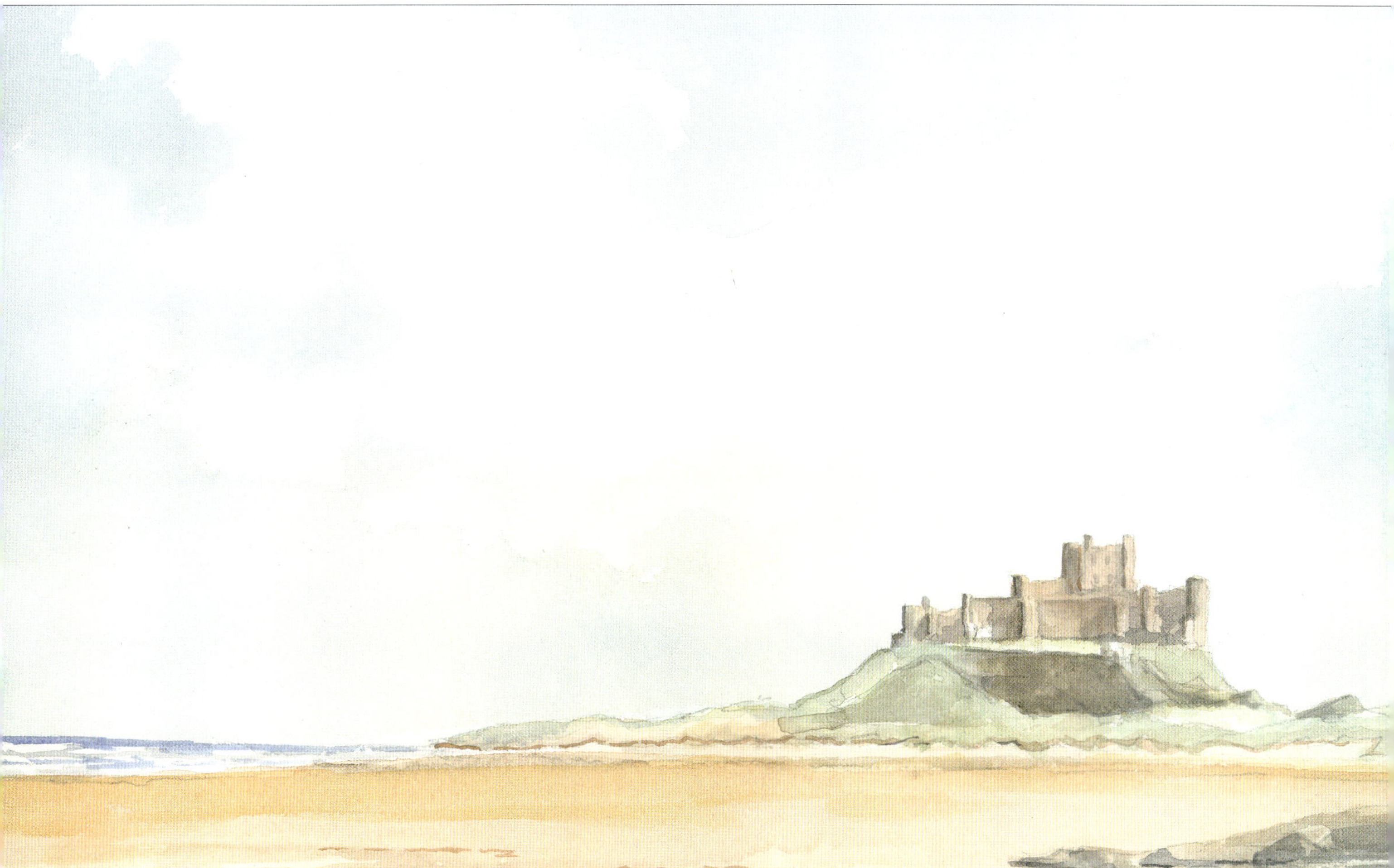

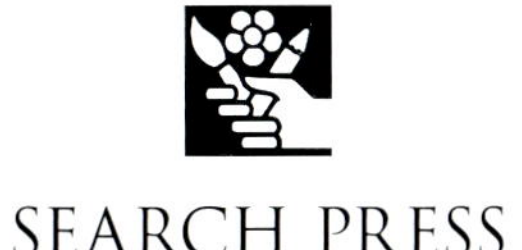

SEARCH PRESS

First published in Great Britain 2011

Search Press Limited
Wellwood, North Farm Road,
Tunbridge Wells, Kent TN2 3DR

Photographs by Debbie Patterson at Search Press studios

ISBN: 978-1-84448-656-4

Suppliers
If you have any difficulty obtaining any of the materials and equipment mentioned in this book, please visit the Search Press website: www.searchpress.com

Publisher's note
All the step-by-step photographs in this book feature the author, Tony Cowlishaw, demonstrating his watercolour painting techniques. No models have been used.

Please note: When removing the perforated sheets of tracing paper from the book, score them first, then carefully pull out each sheet.

Printed in China

Dedication

To my wife Shirley, for her support and encouragement during the preparation of this book.

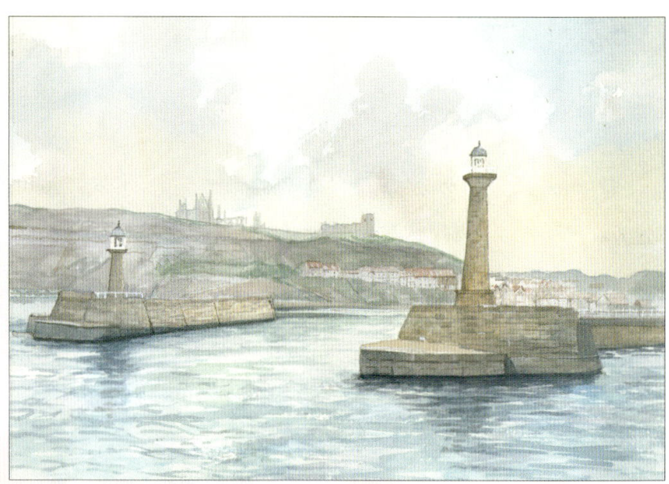

Acknowledgements

I would like to thank Roz Dace for giving me the opportunity to produce this book; also to Edd Ralph, my editor, for his invaluable assistance and patience. Debbie Patterson was the photographer whose expertise produced the excellent photographs. Finally, to all at Search Press who have made this book possible.

Page 1

Bamburgh Castle

56 x 38cm (22 x 15in)

Bamburgh Castle lies in a beautiful isolated location on the Northumberland coast of the UK, overlooking the sea.

Above

Whitby Harbour

42 x 29.5cm (16½ x 11⅝in)

The eye moves from the water in the foreground towards the lighthouse on the right, which forms the focal point of this painting, with its view of the inner harbour and town.

Opposite

Inner Harbour, Port Isaac, Cornwall

42 x 29.5cm (16½ x 11⅝in)

The painting is bisected by the inner harbour wall. The fishing boats below and the cliffs on the right complete this beautiful composition.

Contents

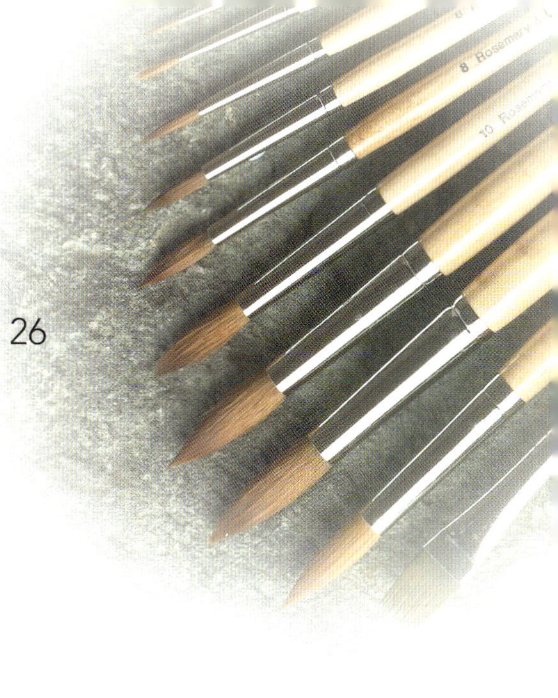

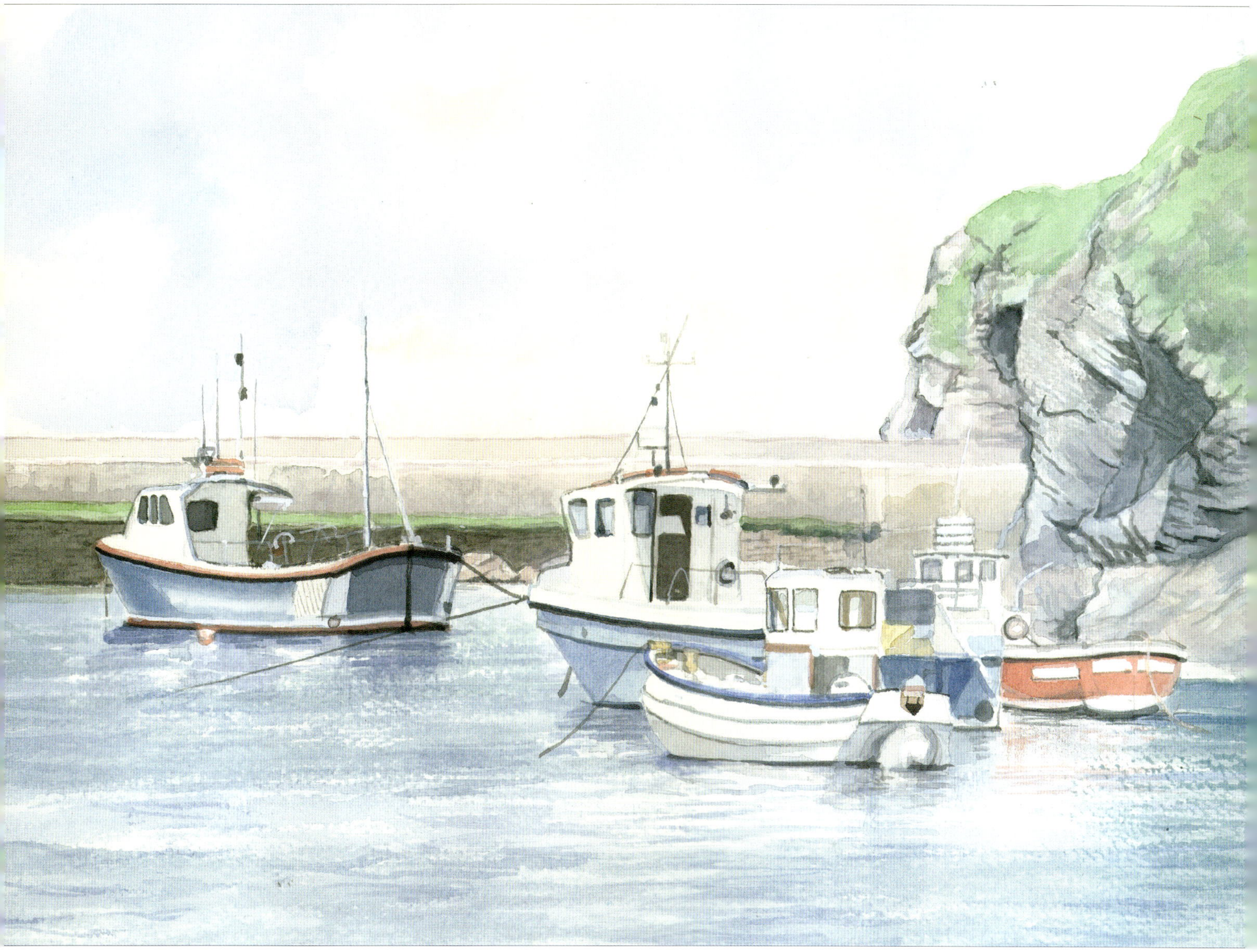

Introduction

The chance to produce a book on the subject of coastal landscapes is very special, as it gives me the opportunity to express my work in a way the amateur painter will understand and emulate. The choice of subjects has been selected to cover a broad spectrum.

The dream of every watercolourist is to produce a unique painting; something special which they may not have previously painted. Although this can be achieved by plenty of practice painting the subject in mind, in order to realise their ultimate dream work of art there are many external factors to be considered.

The main difficulty facing the amateur artist visiting a coastal area is that they may be overwhelmed by the vista which they see and wish to paint. The first challenge is to define the viewpoint they choose for their painting, and this hurdle is removed with this book, which shows selected viewpoints and provides a tracing for each of the five projects, plus a bonus tracing of the painting opposite. The second challenge is to decide how the viewpoint will be painted. I believe that any painting should be divided into components, and the painting of each part should be carefully planned. I have used this method to teach watercolour painting at workshops throughout the country and also in this series of demonstrations.

We are all familiar with the changing tides on the coastline and take them very much for granted. However, as artists our approach is different, as our minds are focused on producing an image of the subject in question which fulfils our own criteria, such as the use of light, time of day and the changing sea level. If the subject is of an inner harbour with a uniform depth of water throughout, changes in the tide may be less noticeable, apart from the changeable height of any vessels in the water and their relationship to the surroundings. If you decide to paint the coastal subject directly *in situ*, always do a sketch of the scene you are painting, as the elements will change: you can then refer to your sketch as reference, especially with regards to changing tides and light conditions.

Once a suitable viewpoint has been chosen, composition of the piece is the first consideration – we look at balance of the subject matter – placement of key features of the composition to catch the eye so that the eye roams throughout the painting to absorb other features, all integral with the main feature. Part of the composition is the use of colour and contrast to separate the main features into an agreeable form.

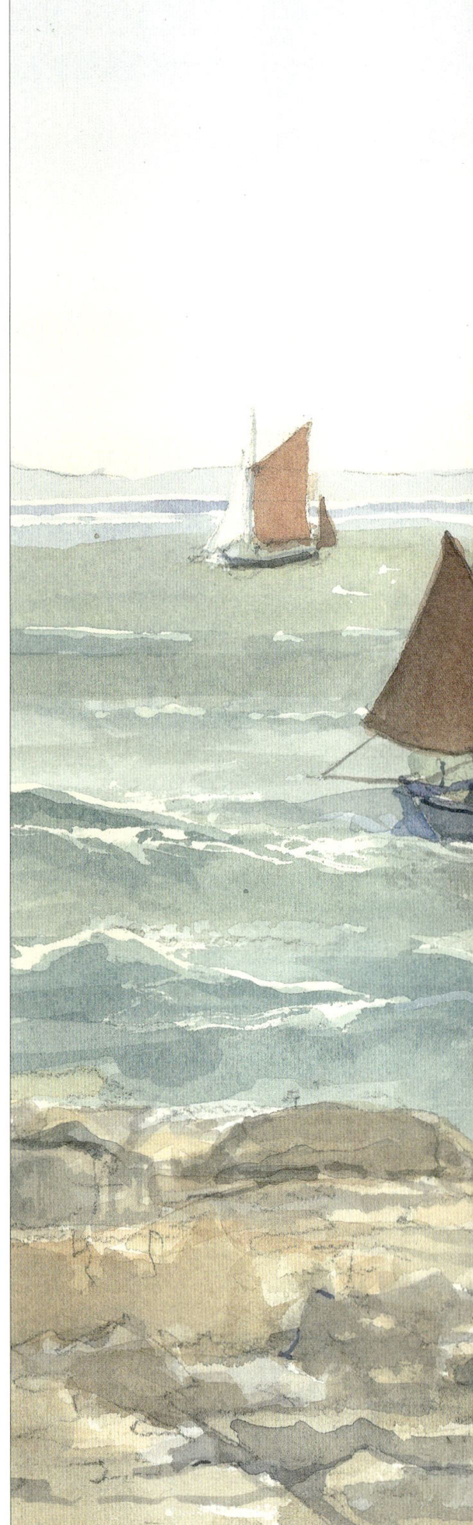

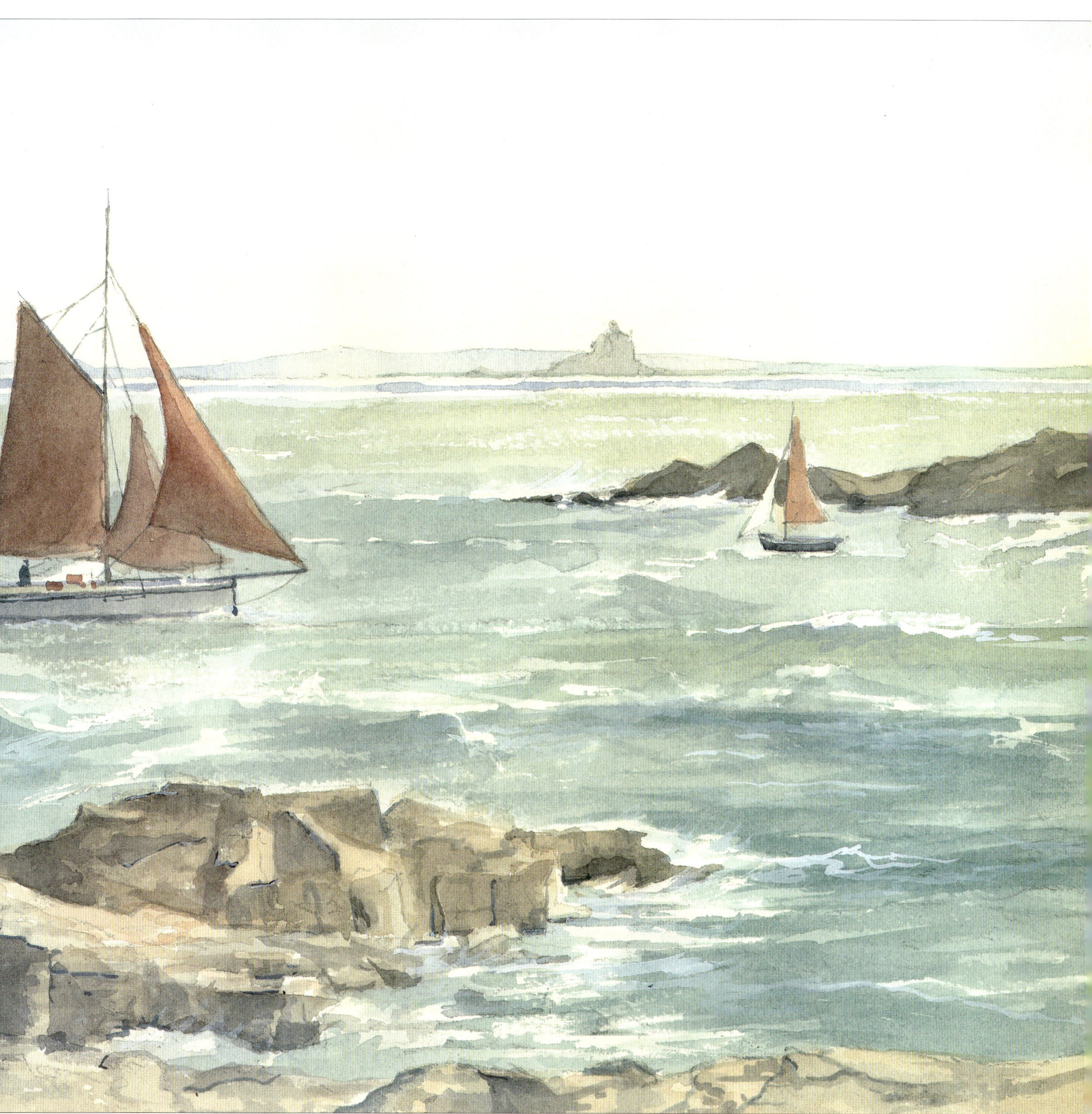

Towards Marazion

42 x 29.5cm (16½ x 11⅝in)

The distant form of St Michael's Mount, in Cornwall, UK, is the focal point of this painting. Use the tracing provided to produce the composition. Apply masking fluid to the wave formation. Use delicate shades of blue-green mixes to define the colours of the sea.

TRACING 6

Materials

A watercolour painting has to be carefully planned. Not only is the composition of the piece planned but the corresponding pigments are chosen and a decision is made about how they will be applied to the paper. The amateur painter should always try and use the best quality materials they can afford; they will make such a difference to the final result.

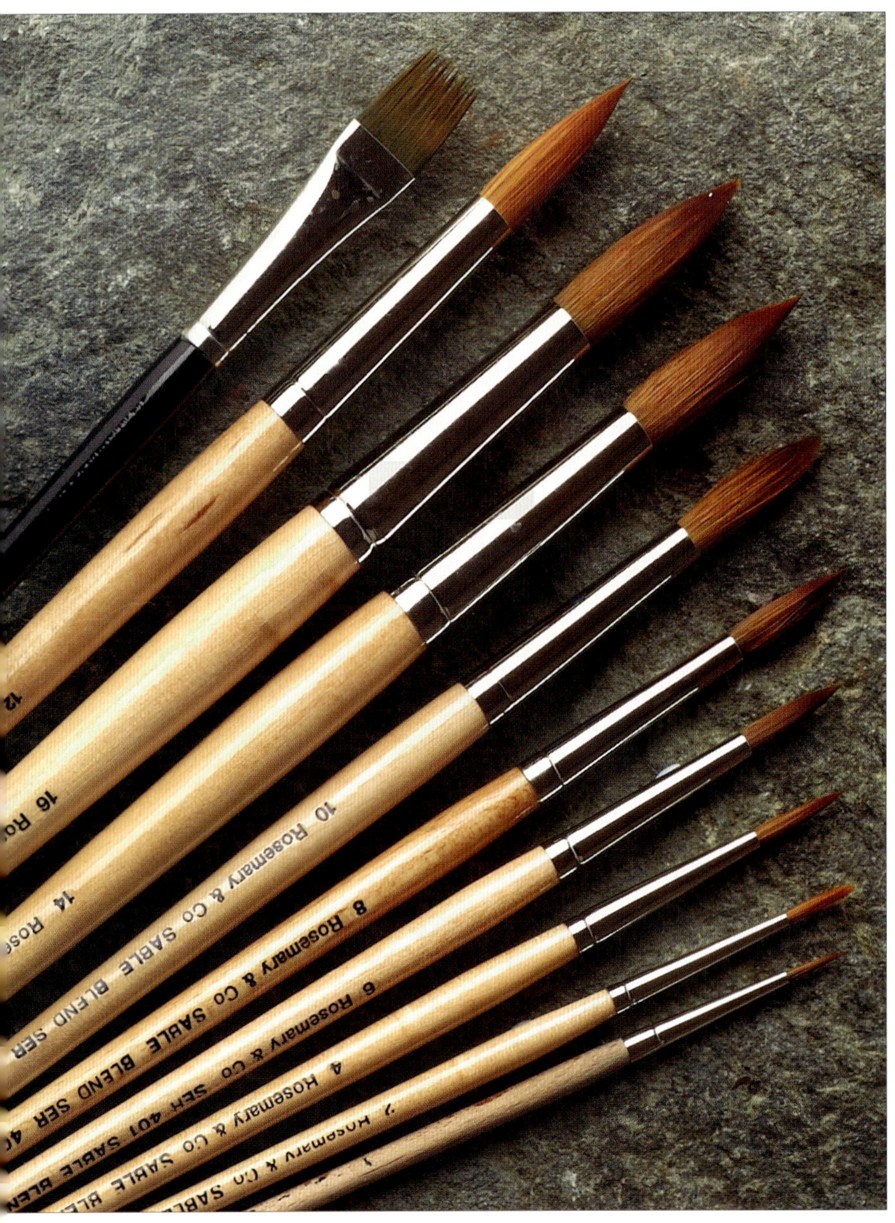

The brushes I have used in this book. From top: 12mm (½in) series 2250 Comber; sizes 12, 16; 14; 10; 8; 6; 4; 2 and 1 series 401 sable/synthetic brushes.

Brushes

I always use round brushes, as I find they give me more control over the applied brushes, but some people favour flat bristle brushes. Both are graded in a similar fashion and can be used for layering washes on the paper. Use of these different types of brushes is mainly left to the preference of the artist and the individual techniques that they employ. Try several types and brands of brushes until you find the variety which suits your technique.

I like to use Kolinsky Sable brushes which are much more durable than the cheaper alternatives. I always favour brushes made by Rosemary & Co, and have used their series 401 brushes in this series of demonstrations, They are of the highest quality and are within the budget of the amateur painter. These have a blend of sable and nylon strands, making them the most versatile of artists' brushes. The sable hairs hold the wash while the nylon gives the brush spring and durability. The sizes range from size 1 through to size 16, and all are round-pointed brushes.

I generally use a size 1 or 2 for the fine work and size 4, 6, 8, 10, 12 and 16 round brushes for the general washes. It is advisable to keep the brushes in pristine condition by washing them well and drawing the bristles forward after use to keep the point sharp.

I have also used a 12mm (½in) series 2250 Comber. It is made by Rosemary & Co and is a specialist brush with some bristles longer than others to produce the effect of grasses within the painting. Look for similar qualities in the brush you select.

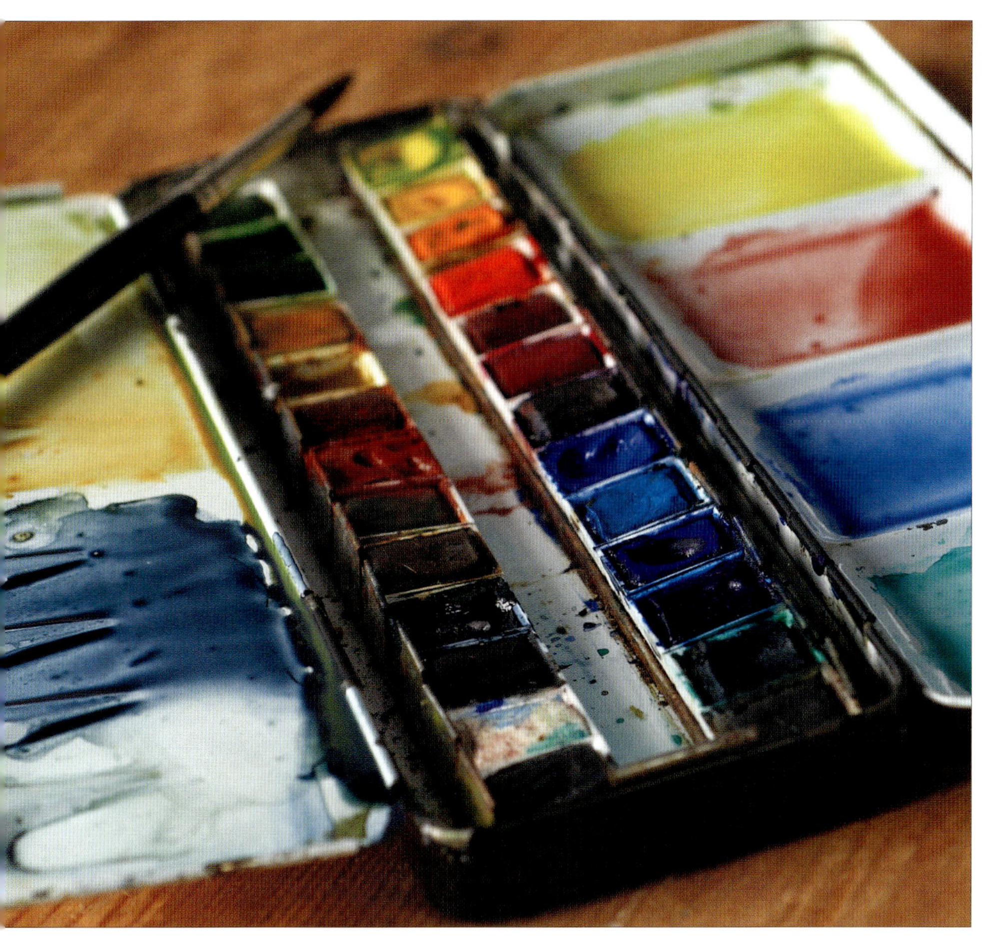

Paints

The choice of watercolour paints is very much based on an individual artist's experience, but I always favour Winsor & Newton's Artists' quality paints as I have used them for many years with great success. Try and buy the best quality pigments that you can afford.

Watercolour paints are available in both pan and tube form, and I would recommend that you try both to find which you prefer.

The colours I use in this book are: French ultramarine, cobalt blue, cerulean blue, Payne's grey, raw sienna, Winsor yellow, Winsor violet, cadmium yellow, cadmium red, Winsor green, burnt umber, ivory black, Indian red, alizarin crimson and viridian.

My palette, made up of pans of watercolour paint.

Paper

There are several types of watercolour paper which determine the quality and textures used by the artist. The surfaces available are Not (short for not hot-pressed), Rough and Smooth (also known as HP or hot-pressed). There are also different weights, or thicknesses of standard watercolour paper: 190gsm (90lb) being the thinnest and lightest and 640gsm (300lb) the thickest and heaviest. Generally speaking, the lighter papers should be stretched before use, but this is dependant on the size of the painting for which the paper is being prepared. In addition to texture and weight, a variety of various tinted papers are available, which can be used for specialist purposes.

Paper can be readily purchased from good art material supply shops in convenient pads, but large sheets can be purchased and cut to size. This is a more economical approach, especially if bought in bulk.

I favour the use of Saunders Waterford 640gsm (300lb) Not paper, which is manufactured by St Cuthbert's Mill.

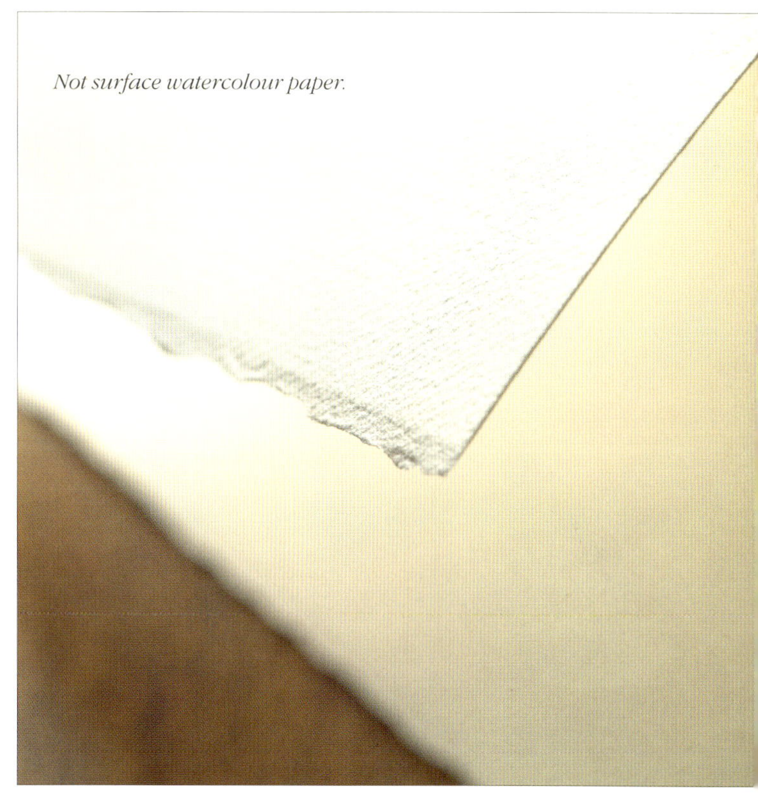

Not surface watercolour paper.

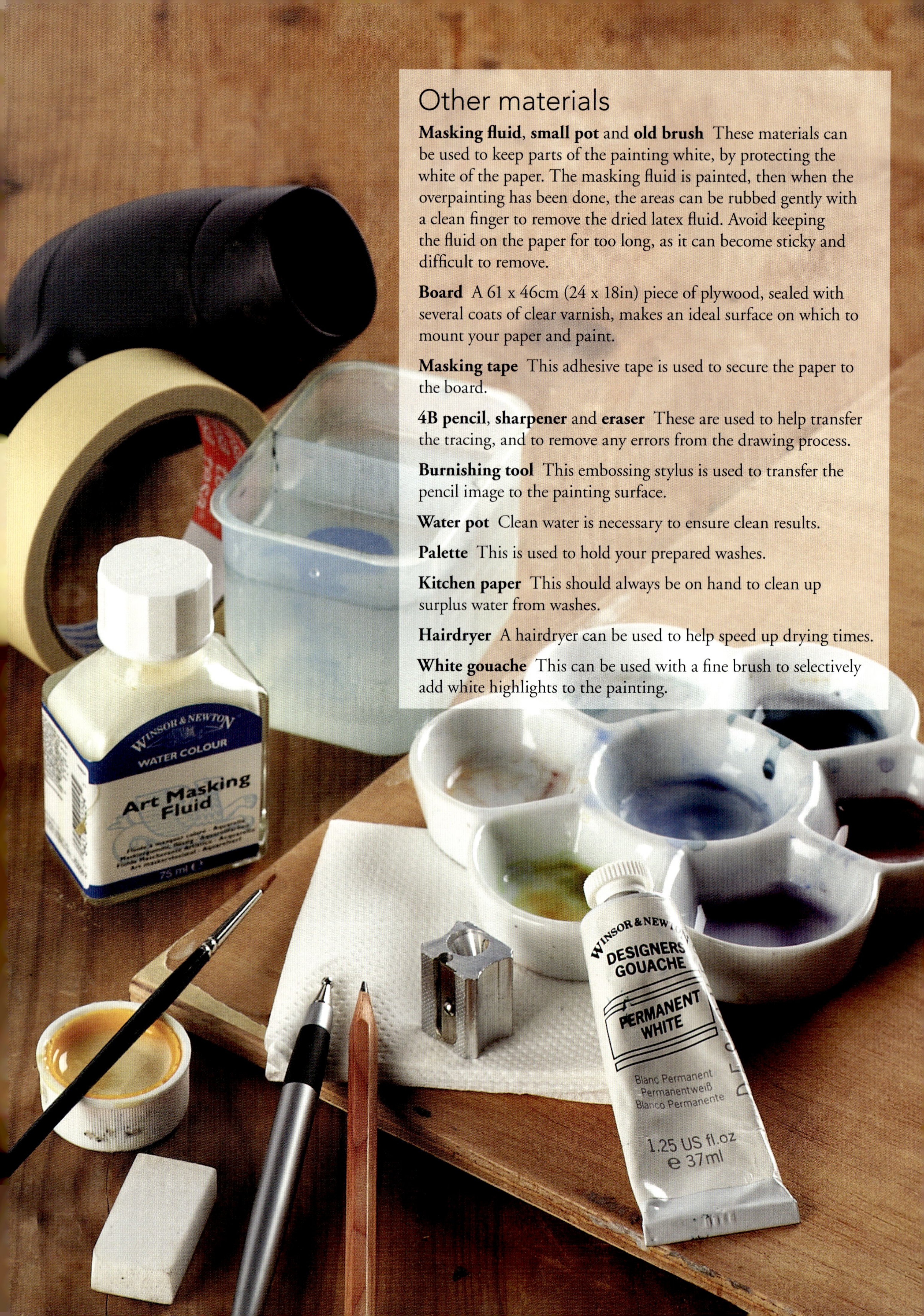

Other materials

Masking fluid, **small pot** and **old brush** These materials can be used to keep parts of the painting white, by protecting the white of the paper. The masking fluid is painted, then when the overpainting has been done, the areas can be rubbed gently with a clean finger to remove the dried latex fluid. Avoid keeping the fluid on the paper for too long, as it can become sticky and difficult to remove.

Board A 61 x 46cm (24 x 18in) piece of plywood, sealed with several coats of clear varnish, makes an ideal surface on which to mount your paper and paint.

Masking tape This adhesive tape is used to secure the paper to the board.

4B pencil, **sharpener** and **eraser** These are used to help transfer the tracing, and to remove any errors from the drawing process.

Burnishing tool This embossing stylus is used to transfer the pencil image to the painting surface.

Water pot Clean water is necessary to ensure clean results.

Palette This is used to hold your prepared washes.

Kitchen paper This should always be on hand to clean up surplus water from washes.

Hairdryer A hairdryer can be used to help speed up drying times.

White gouache This can be used with a fine brush to selectively add white highlights to the painting.

Transferring the image

Tracings are provided at the front of this book for all the demonstration paintings, and a bonus tracing is provided for the painting on page 5. You can reuse each tracing several times so you can use the same basic image to produce two quite different paintings. Extract the tracing you wish to use from the front of the book and follow the instructions below to transfer the image to your watercolour paper.

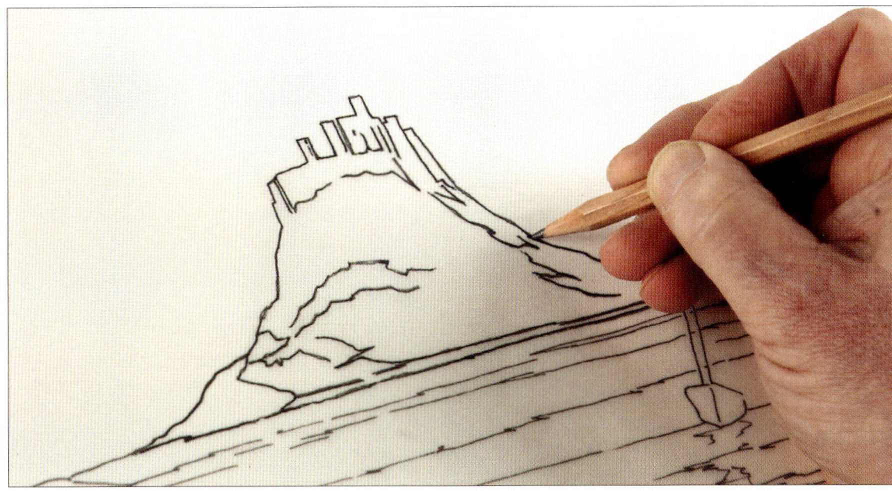

1 Turn the tracing over and draw carefully over the back of the lines with a 4B pencil to produce a crisp, thin line.

2 Tape the tracing face up on your watercolour paper with masking tape. Rub over the lines with a burnishing tool, as shown, to transfer the graphite on to the paper.

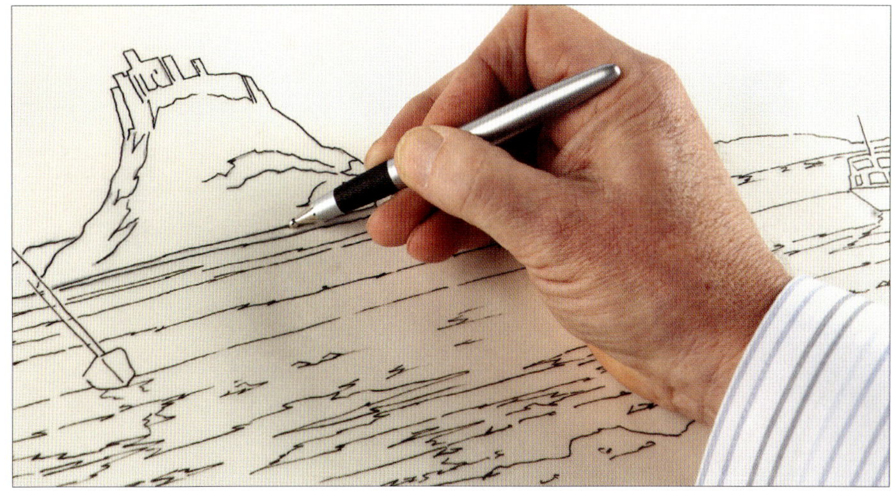

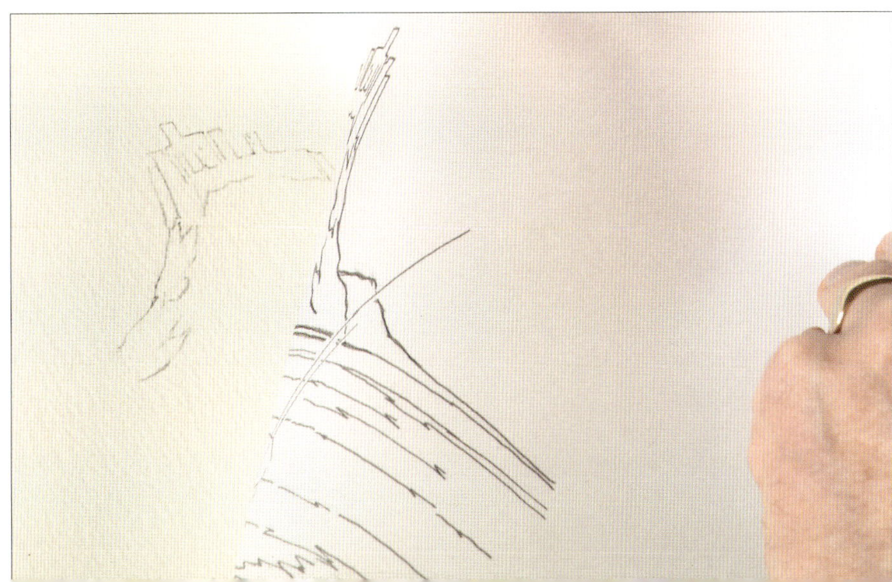

3 You can lift up the tracing as you work to check that the image is being transferred on to the watercolour paper correctly. Once it is all transferred, add any further detail you wish with your pencil. You are ready to begin painting.

Barge in Creek

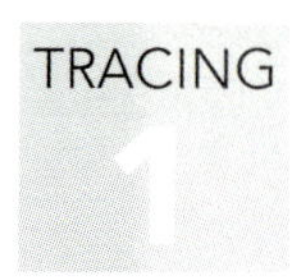

This picture is of an old sailing barge in the evening light. I wanted to capture a dramatic evening sky with the corresponding atmospheric reflections in the water. I have included some pieces of land to the left and right in the foreground so that the eye travels towards the barge, which is positioned in the golden section.

You will need

Saunders Waterford Not 640gsm (300lb) watercolour paper, 56 x 38cm (22 x 15in)

Colours: cobalt blue, raw sienna, Payne's grey, Indian red, alizarin crimson, viridian, ivory black, cerulean blue and Winsor yellow

Brushes: size 16 round, size 8 round, size 6 round, size 2 round and size 1 round

Masking tape and board

Masking fluid and old brush

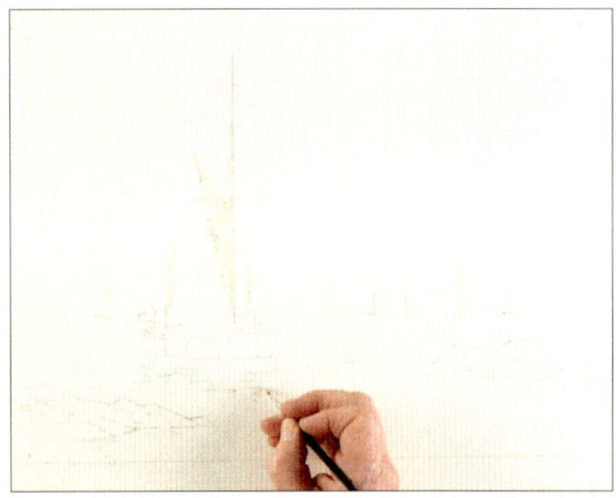

1 Transfer the tracing to the paper following the instructions on page 9, then secure your paper to the board using masking tape run down the edges. Use an old brush to apply masking fluid to the main mast, the sprit and appropriate sails of the barge, as well as some details of the distant yachts and water as shown.

2 Allow the masking fluid to dry, then prepare fairly dilute wells of the following paints: cobalt blue and raw sienna. Use the size 16 round to apply cobalt blue to the top centre of the sky wet-on-dry, working in broad, horizontal strokes.

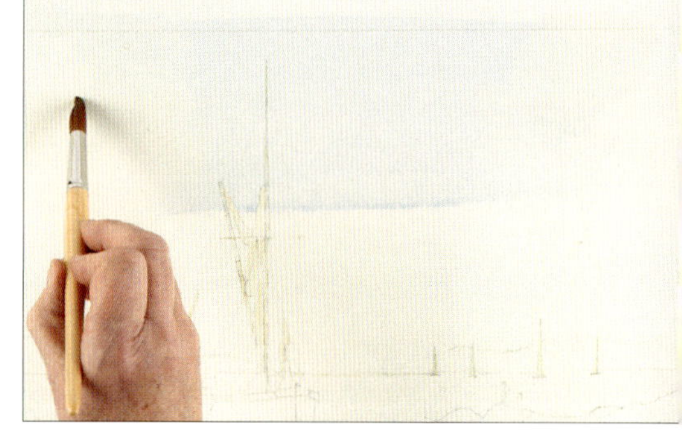

3 Still using the size 16 round, diffuse the colour out to the sides of the painting with clean water.

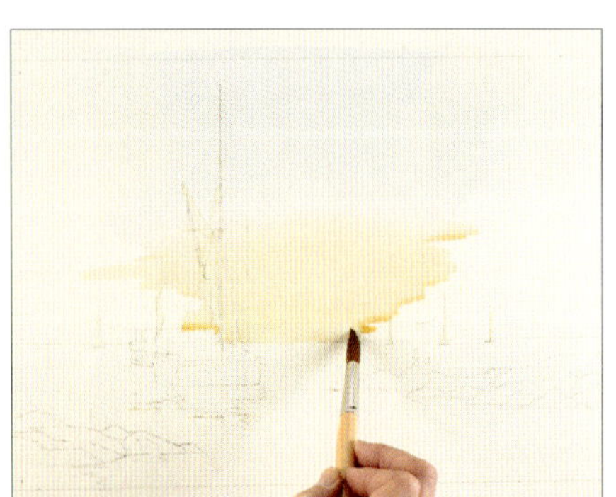

4 Working wet-in-wet, apply dilute raw sienna into the centre of the sky, blending it down from inside the blue area to the horizon, creating a graduated wash.

5 Diffuse the raw sienna out to the sides using clean water, keeping the horizon line clean as shown.

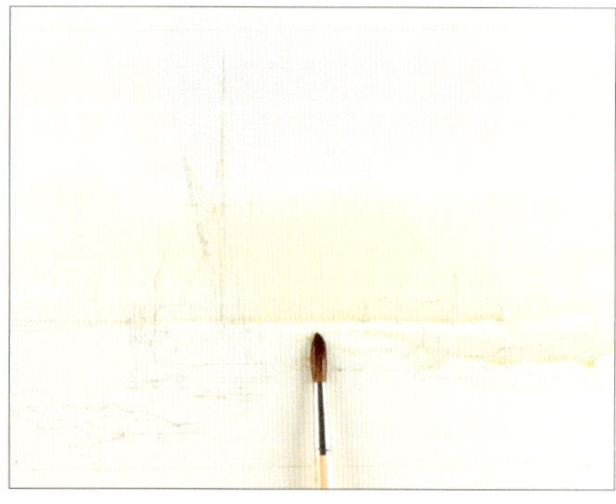

6 Load the size 16 brush with raw sienna, then draw the side of the brush lightly across the top of the water, turning it as you work to release the pigment. This will create a broken effect.

7 Continue creating the broken, sparkling effect by drawing raw sienna across the upper part of the water, and introducing a little cobalt blue at the very bottom of the painting in the same way. Allow to dry thoroughly before continuing.

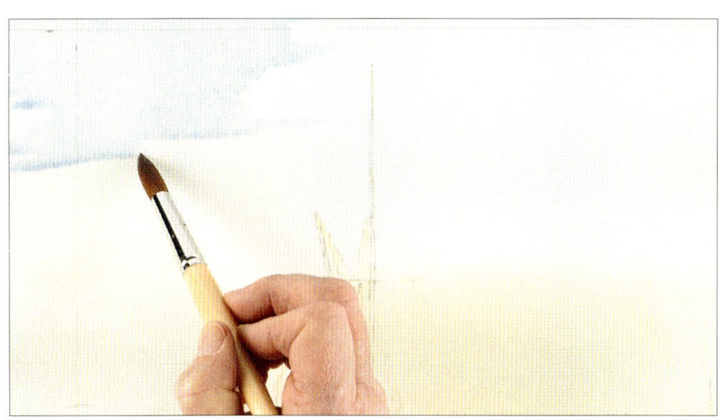

8 Prepare some wells of pure raw sienna, a mix of Payne's grey with cobalt blue and a mix of Indian red and alizarin crimson. Still using the size 16, apply the blue-grey mix in the top left, drawing it horizontally to suggest the edges of cloud formations.

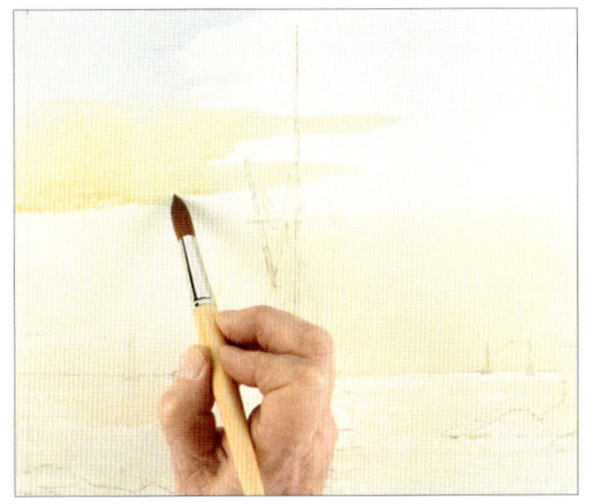

9 Working wet-in-wet, apply horizontal strokes of raw sienna below and into the blue area as shown.

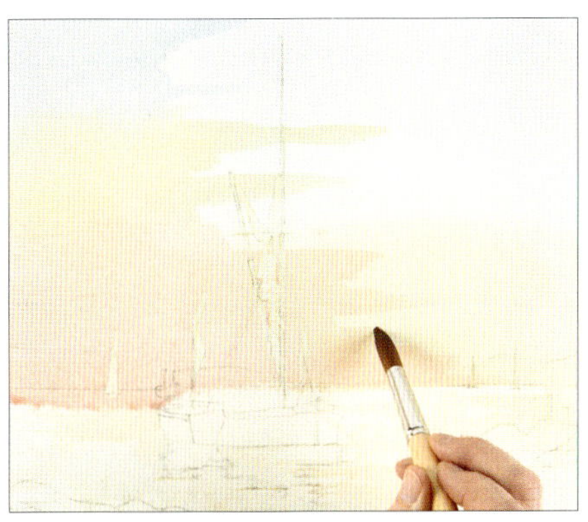

10 Still working wet-in-wet, apply the warm Indian red and alizarin crimson mix below and into the raw sienna down to the horizon.

11 Repeat the process on the right-hand side of the picture, again working down to the horizon.

12 Load the brush with the warm mix (Indian red and alizarin crimson) and draw the side of the brush lightly across the water below the horizon, rotating the brush to release more of the paint.

13 Load the brush with the blue-grey mix (Payne's grey with cobalt blue) and draw the side of the brush lightly across the water below the warm area, again rotating the brush to release the paint.

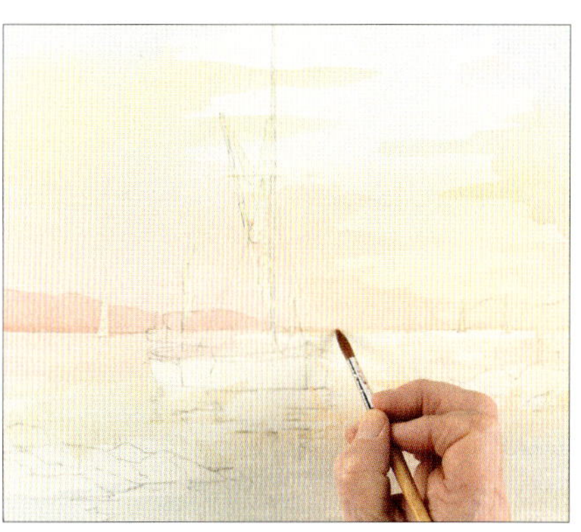

14 Change to the size 8 round brush and paint the distant hills on the left-hand horizon using the warm mix.

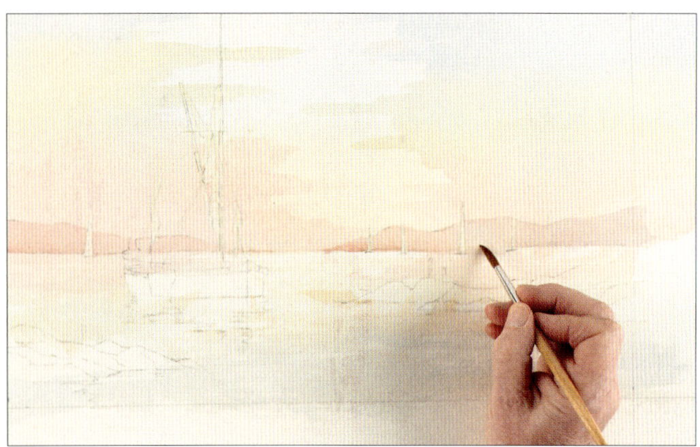

15 Paint the hills on the right-hand side in the same way, working some of the cobalt blue and Payne's grey mix in wet-in-wet on the extreme right.

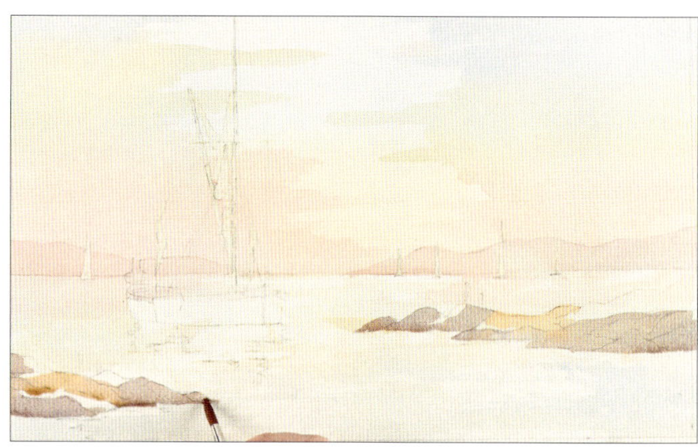

16 Prepare some fairly strong wells of raw sienna and a warm grey mix of Payne's grey and Indian red. Still using the size 8 round, use these two mixes to paint in different areas of the rocks on the right-hand and left-hand sides, leaving a few white gaps.

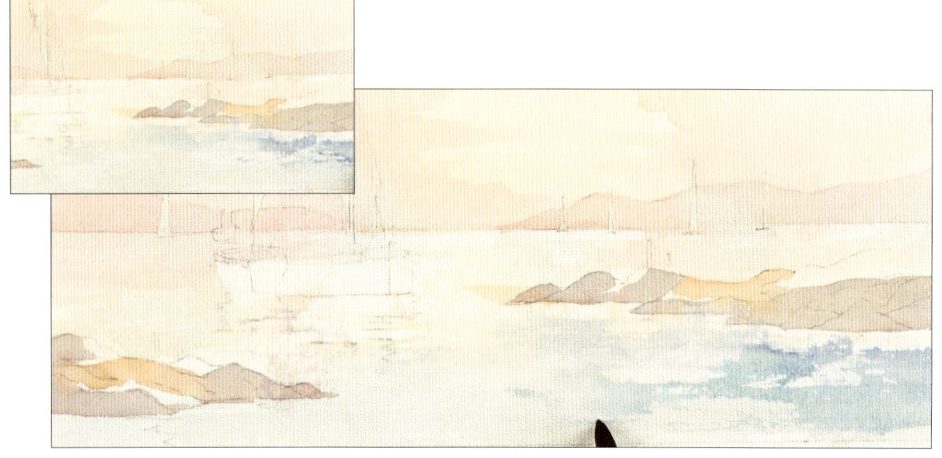

17 Make a mix of Payne's grey with a little cobalt blue and alizarin crimson added. Switch to the size 16 round and use the side of the brush to draw the mix lightly across the foreground sea from the left to the centre (see inset). Turn the brush to release fresh paint. Repeat the process with viridian, again drawing it lightly across the painting from the right to the centre.

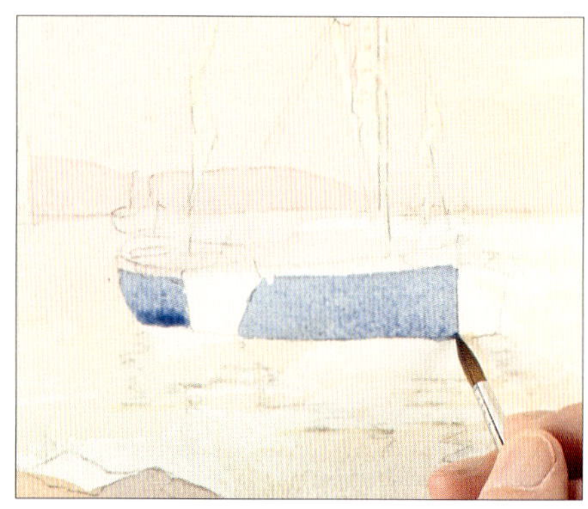

18 Use the size 6 brush to apply a fairly dark mix of cobalt blue and Payne's grey to the left-hand part of the barge's hull.

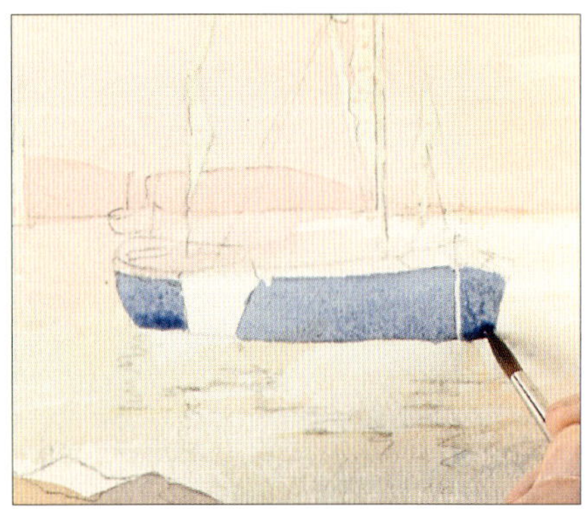

19 Leave a very fine gap at the prow and paint the right-hand part of the barge's hull in the same way.

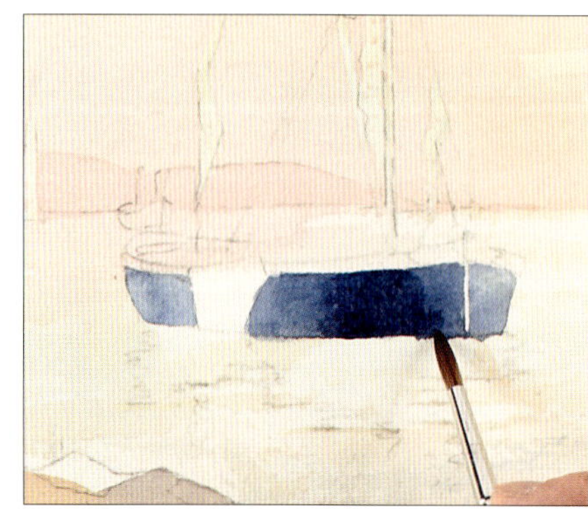

20 While the paint is still wet, add more Payne's grey to the mix and drop in this darker mix to shade the part of the hull on the left of the prow. Allow to dry thoroughly.

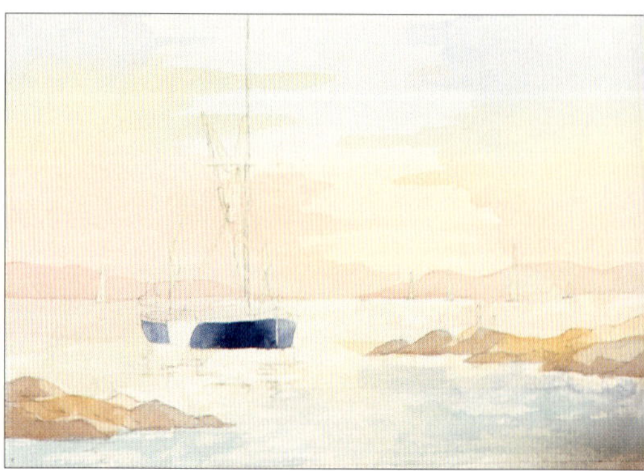

21 Still using the size 6 round, apply raw sienna to the rocks, covering the white areas, then shade the remaining rocks with a glaze of cobalt blue and Payne's grey.

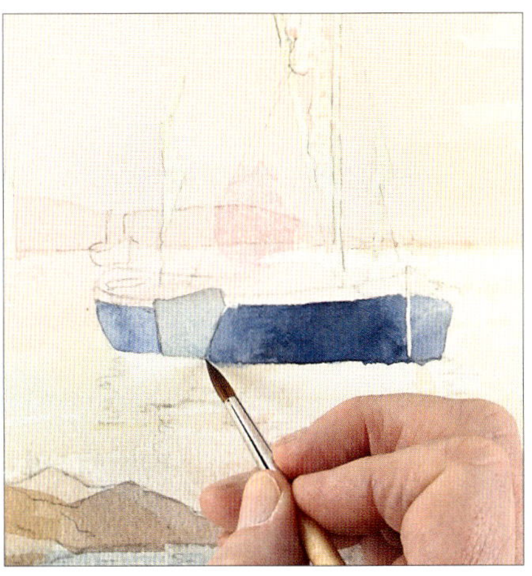

22 Make a dilute mix of ivory black and cerulean blue and paint the leeboard of the boat.

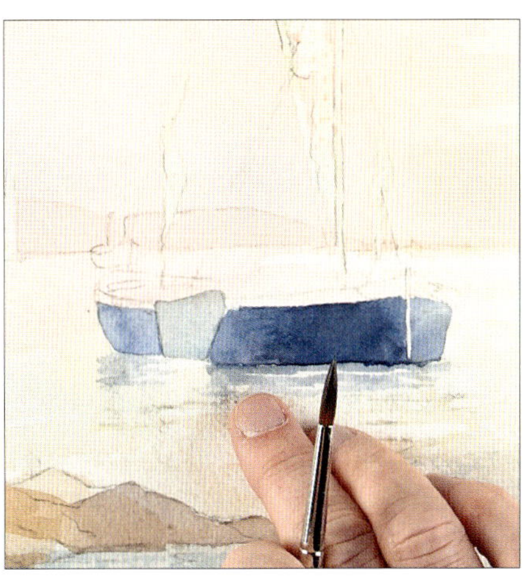

23 Use the cobalt blue and Payne's grey mix to paint some horizontal strokes below the boat as reflections. Draw the wet paint down with your finger.

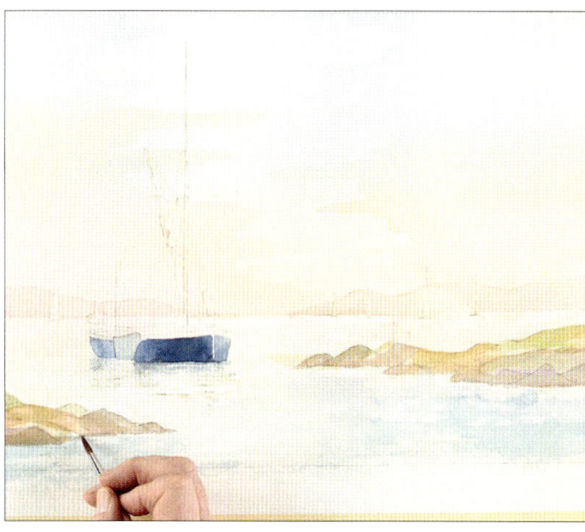

24 Using a mix of raw sienna and viridian, glaze the top of the rocks on both sides.

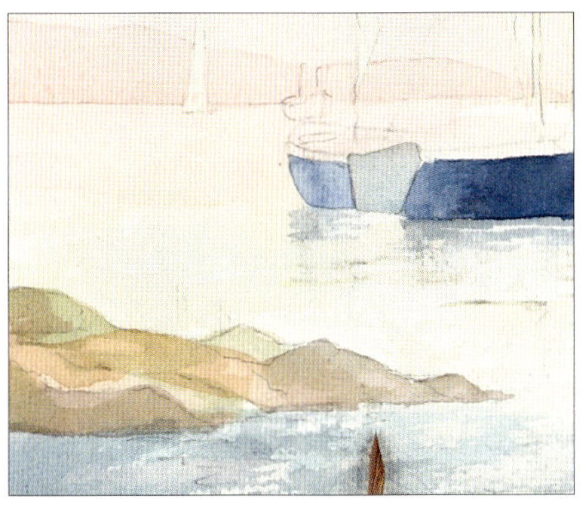

25 Use the side of the brush to draw the cobalt blue and Payne's grey mix lightly over the surface of the water below the rocks to represent their reflections.

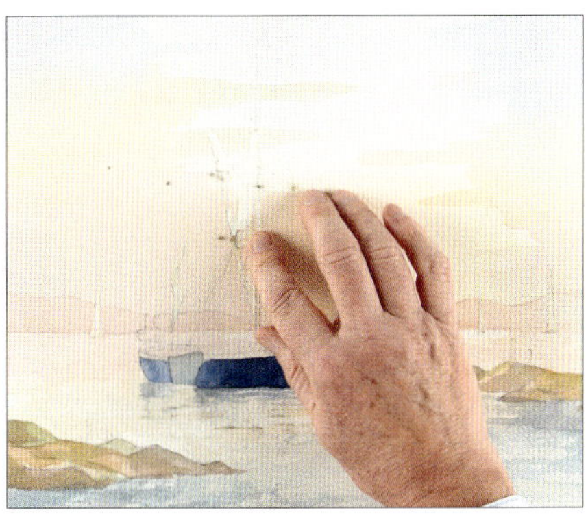

26 Allow the painting to dry completely before proceeding, then use a clean finger to carefully rub away all of the masking fluid.

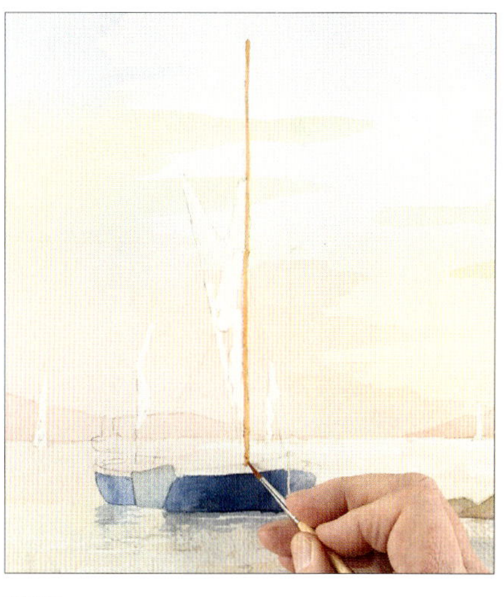

27 Use the size 2 round to paint in the mast using raw sienna with some Indian red added. Draw the paint down in a smooth stroke.

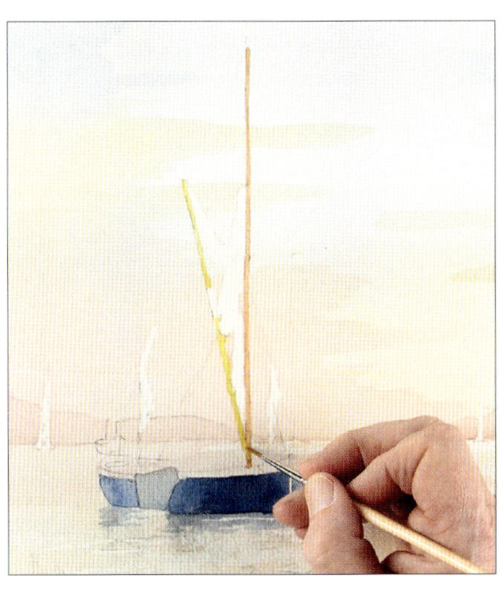

28 Still using the size 2 round, paint in the sprit mast with Winsor yellow. Leave the central area white as shown.

29 Paint the reflections with slightly stronger mixes of the same colours. Make a zigzag stroke, then draw the paint downwards as you get further from the boat.

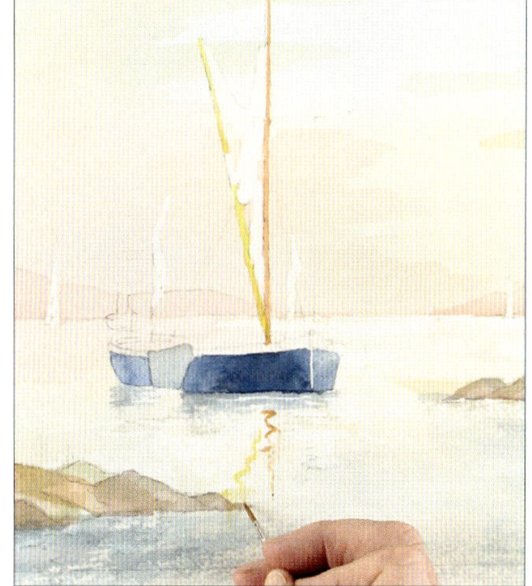

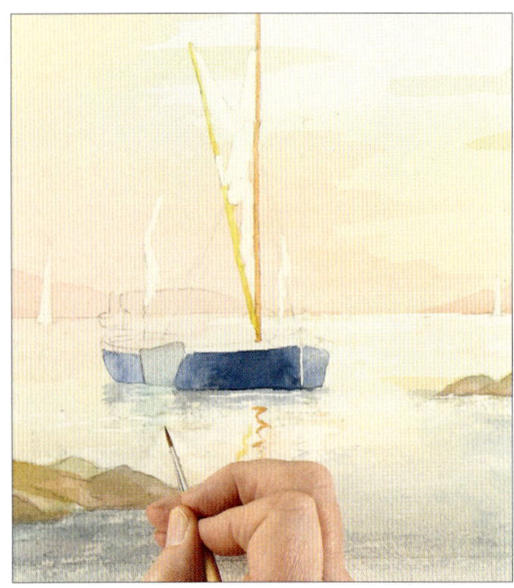

30 Paint the reflections of the leeboard with a mix of cerulean blue and ivory black.

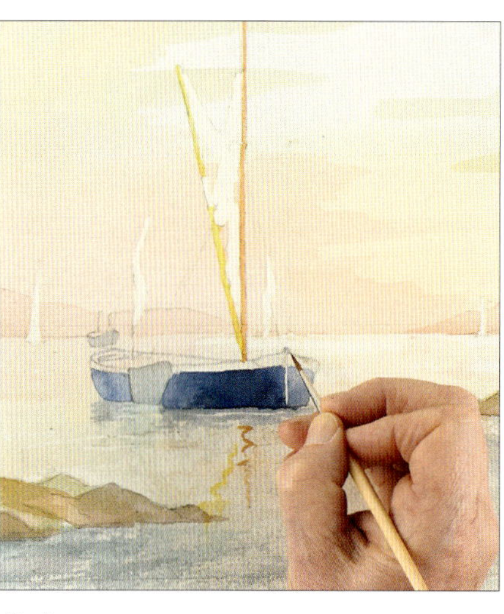

31 Use the cobalt blue and Payne's grey mix to paint the lifeboat behind the main vessel. Use the same mix to paint in the structure of the top of the barge's hull.

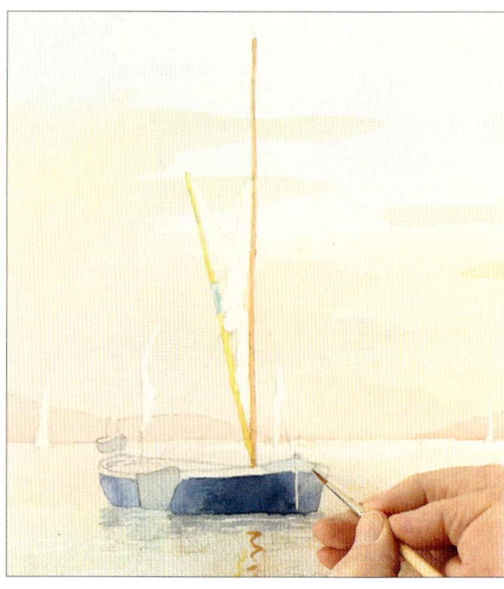

32 Paint the central area of the sprit mast, the top of the main mast and the top of the hull with cerulean blue.

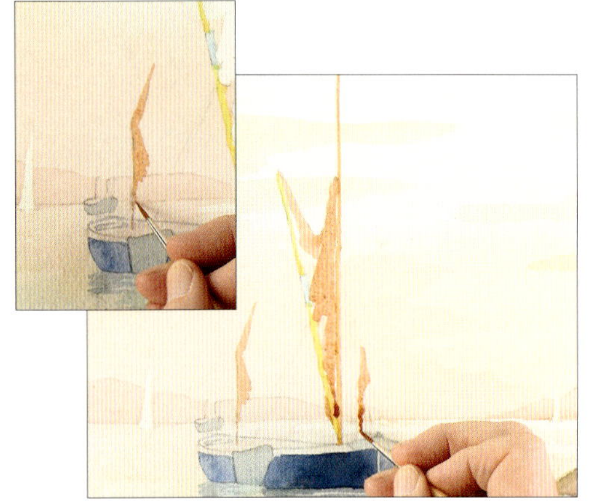

33 Add a hint of raw sienna to Indian red and paint the sail at the aft of the barge using the size 2 brush (see inset), then paint the furled sail and the sail at the prow.

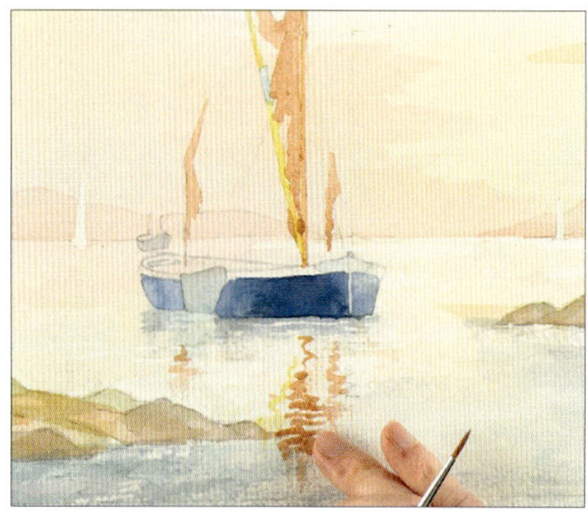

34 Add the reflections of the sail with the same brush and paint mix, making a small zigzag and drawing the paint downwards with your finger.

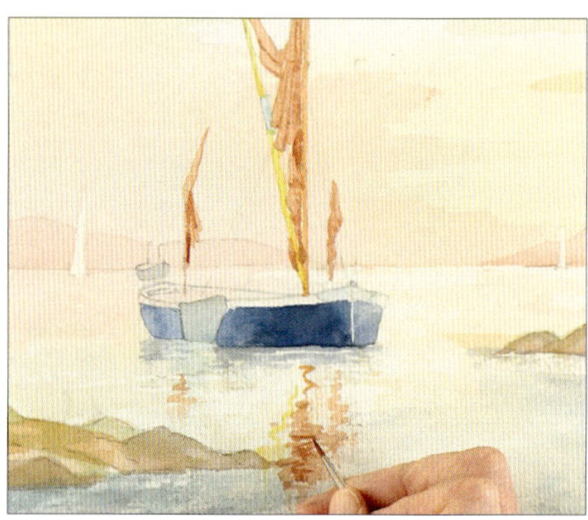

35 Add folds to the sails and reflections with pure Indian red.

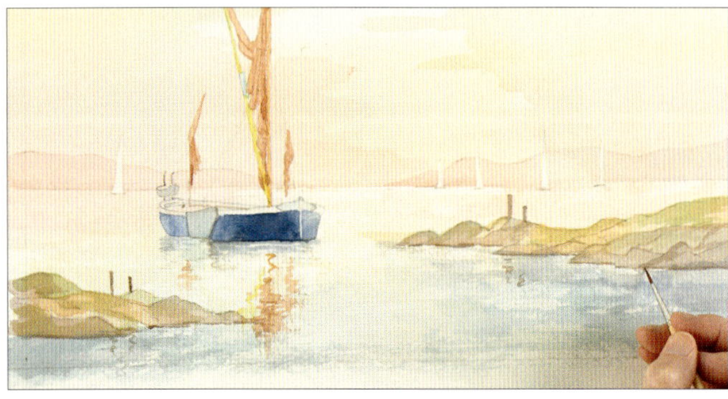

36 Mix Payne's grey with a little Indian red to paint in the hulls of the background vessels, the foreground mooring posts and their reflections, then add some strokes of the mix between the land and the water, and on the rocks to develop their texture.

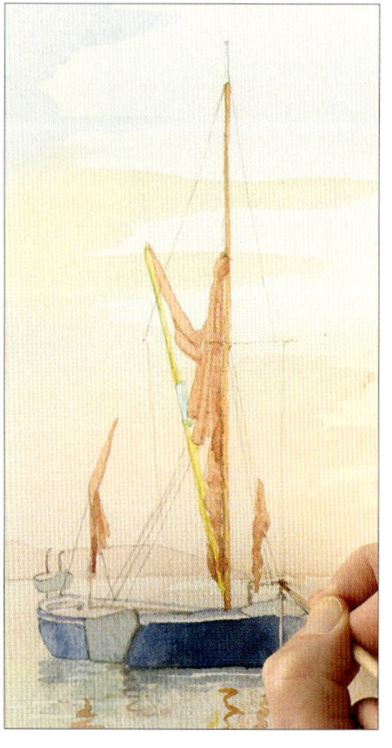

37 Paint the top of the hull with cobalt blue, then use the tip of the size 1 round with the same mix to paint in the rigging. Work carefully and as cleanly as you can, using as few strokes as possible. Use the same mix, brush and technique to add shading to the masts on the left.

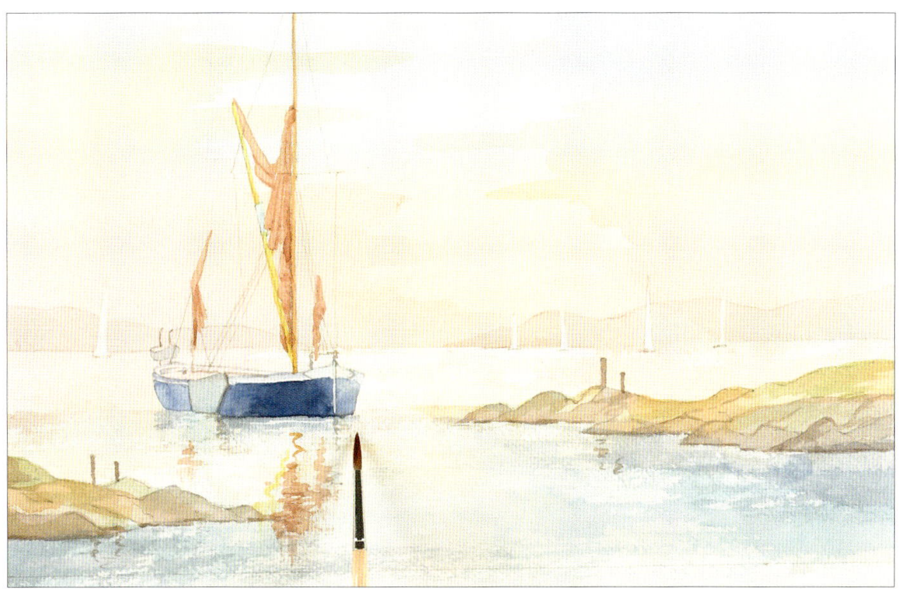

38 Working from the left of the painting towards the barge, draw Indian red with a touch of Payne's grey across the surface using the side of the size 8 round. Repeat very lightly from the end of the right-hand rocks towards the barge.

39 Mix viridian with Payne's grey and enhance the wash in the foreground by dragging the side of the brush from the edges towards the centre, and also under the barge as a reflection.

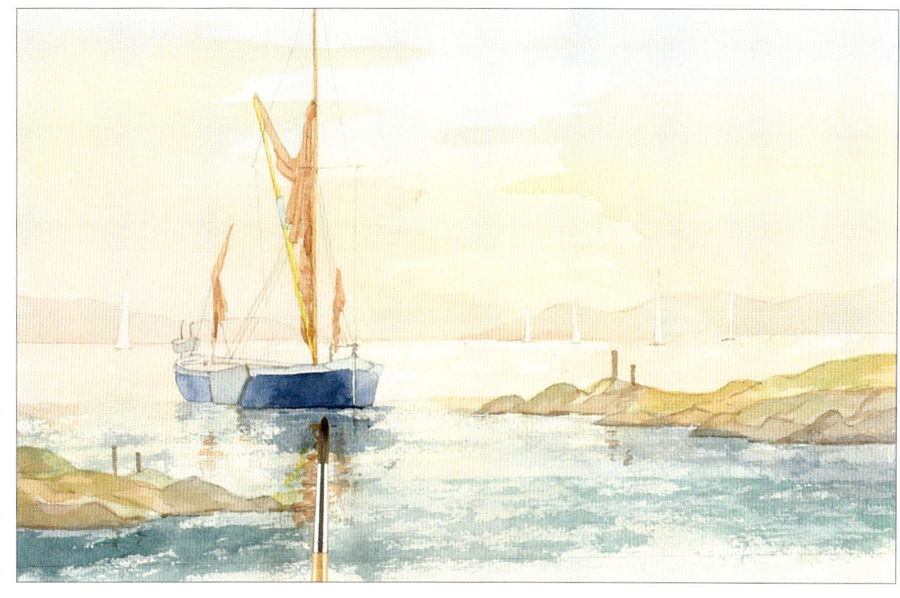

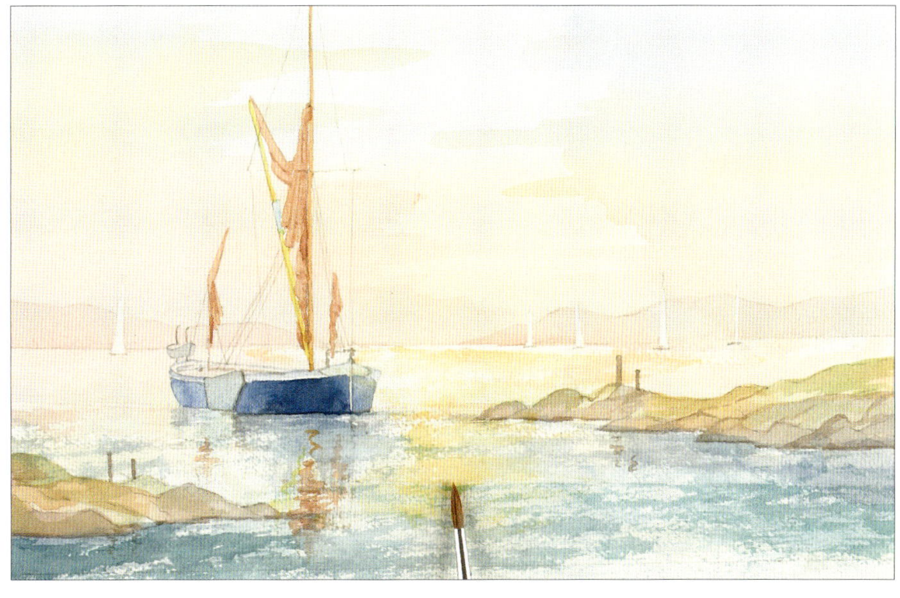

40 Add a little raw sienna to Winsor yellow and repeat the process over the background water, drawing it into the centre as shown.

Overleaf
The finished painting.

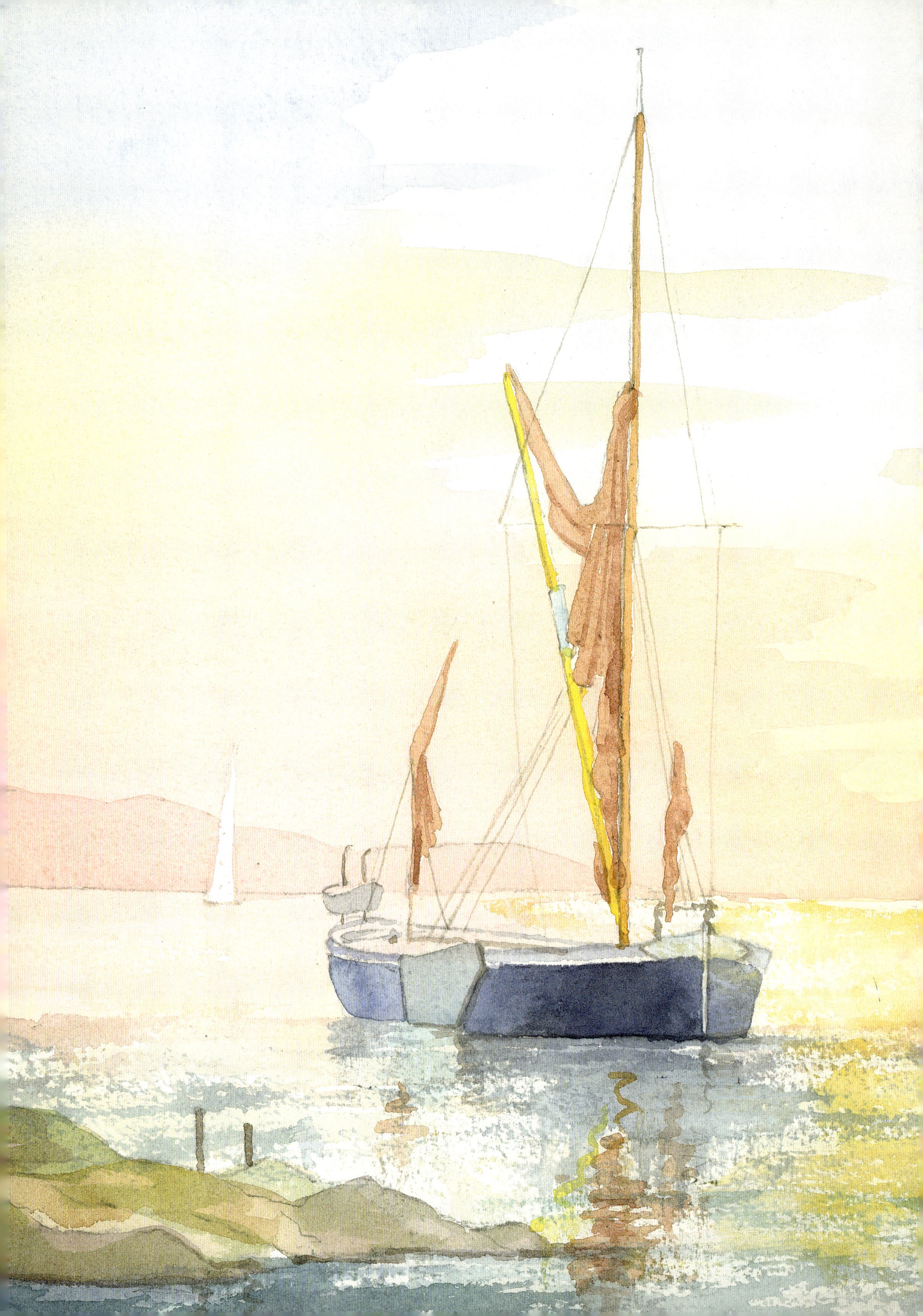

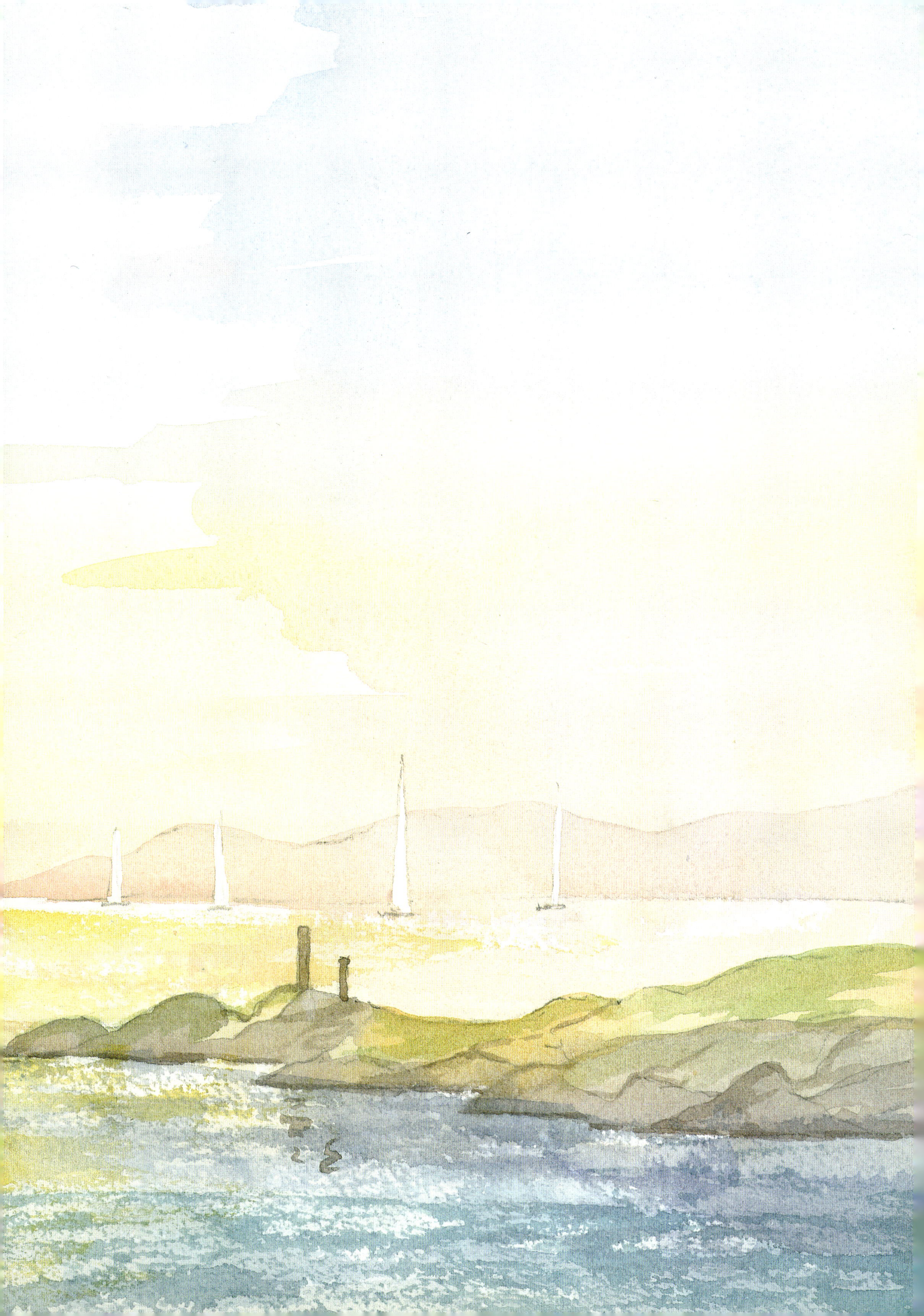

Lindisfarne Castle

TRACING 2

This dramatic castle provides a strong counterpoint to the sea and sky in this example, occupying the golden section and providing a fantastic focal point. The painting is divided into various components: a dramatic sky, the castle, the water and the foreground; and each is important to the composition as a whole. The water reflects the view, together with some small boats to add secondary points of interest, and the foreground binds the whole painting together. The light source is on the right-hand side. Work through each section in turn to be sure of a cohesive finished painting.

You will need

Saunders Waterford Not 640gsm (300lb) watercolour paper, 56 x 38cm (22 x 15in)

Colours: cobalt blue, raw sienna, Payne's grey, Winsor violet, French ultramarine, Winsor yellow, cobalt blue, Indian red, viridian and cerulean blue

Brushes: size 16 round, size 6 round, size 2 round, size 8 round and size 1 round

Masking tape and board

Masking fluid and old brush

1 Transfer the tracing to the paper following the instructions on page 9, then secure your paper to the board using masking tape run down the edges. Use an old brush to apply masking fluid to the sailing vessels, including the masts, and also the stony areas in the foreground, as shown.

2 Prepare wells of pure cobalt blue and raw sienna with a touch of cobalt blue. Use the size 16 to apply a wash of cobalt blue to the whole sky, working downwards from the top of the picture to the level of the castle. Use the side of the brush, turning it as you work to release the paint and give an irregular edge.

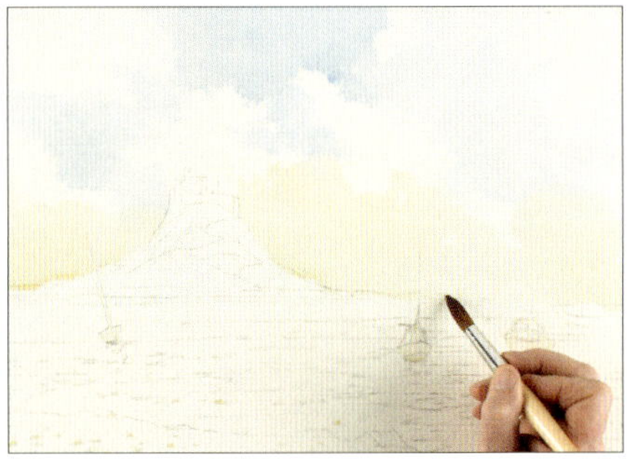

3 Apply the raw sienna and cobalt blue mix in the same way, working wet-in-wet from slightly above the level of the castle to the horizon. Aim to blend the two colours together to produce a rich grey effect in the sky. Allow the paint to dry completely before continuing.

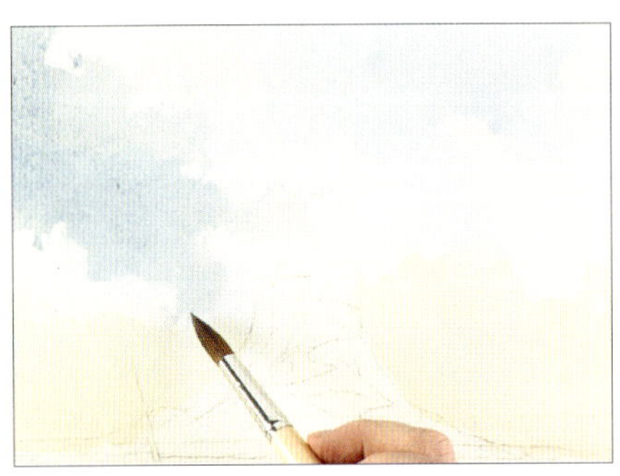

4 Mix Payne's grey into the cobalt blue well, and apply this at the top left as a glaze over the blue area of the sky.

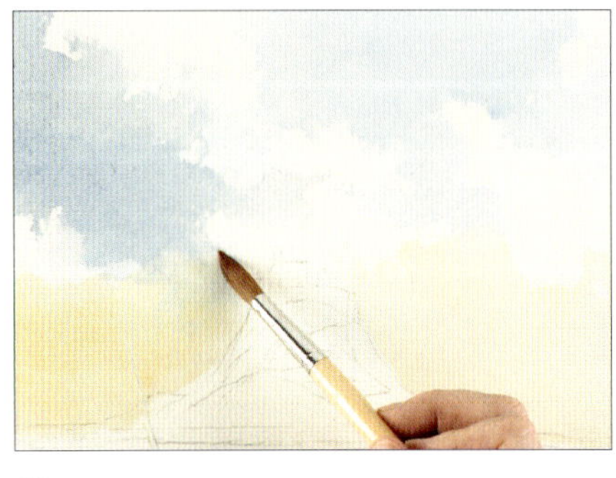

5 Working wet-in-wet, glaze the lower part of the sky on the left with pure raw sienna, working it up into the new blue glaze.

6 Glaze the right-hand and central areas of the sky with the same mixes and techniques.

7 Using the mix of raw sienna with a touch of cobalt blue, draw the side of the size 16 round brush lightly across the water in the midground to create the reflections of the sky, turning the brush as you work to release the paint.

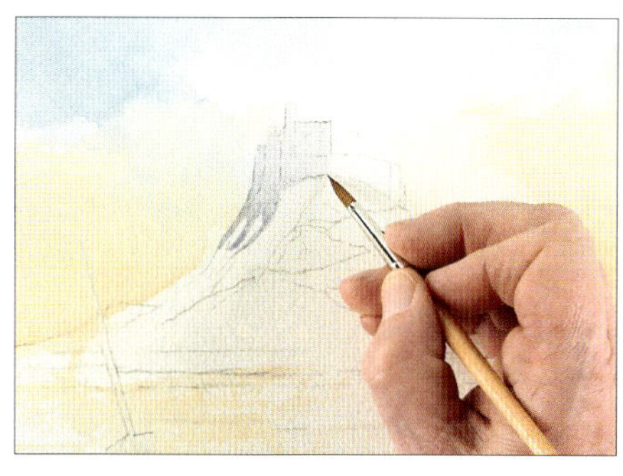

8 Start to paint the castle using the size 6 round and a mix of Payne's grey and Winsor violet, concentrating on the shaded side. This is on the left-hand side as the subject is illuminated from the right.

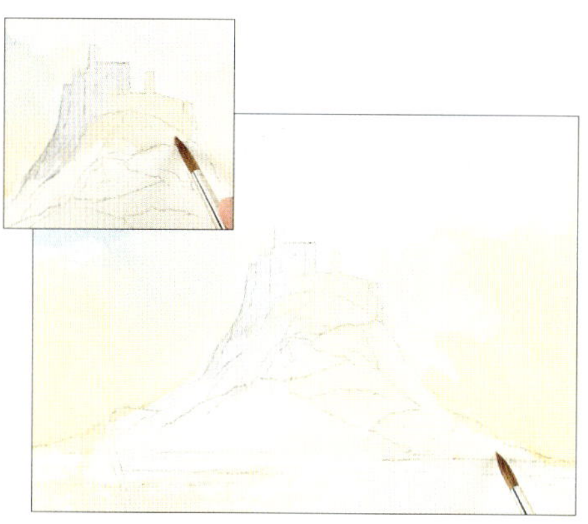

9 Work raw sienna on to the right-hand side of the castle to show the light, allowing the colour to flow into the shaded side (see inset). Work down the hill beneath the castle with the same colours.

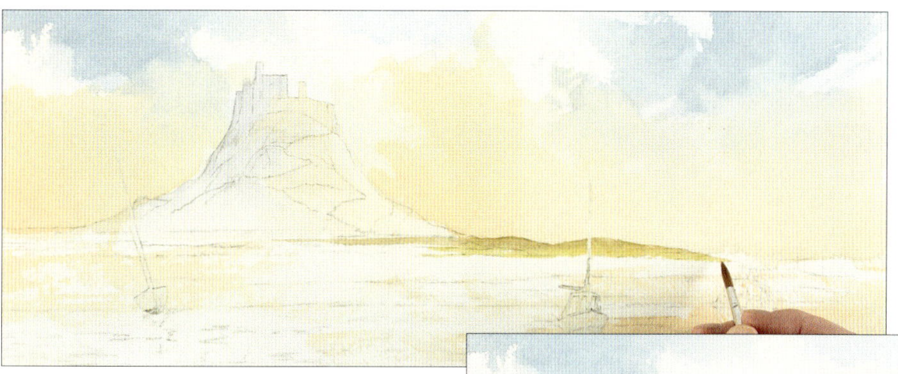

10 Create a green mix from French ultramarine and raw sienna, and use the tip of the size 6 brush to establish the horizon line. Vary the colour with some Winsor yellow beneath the line.

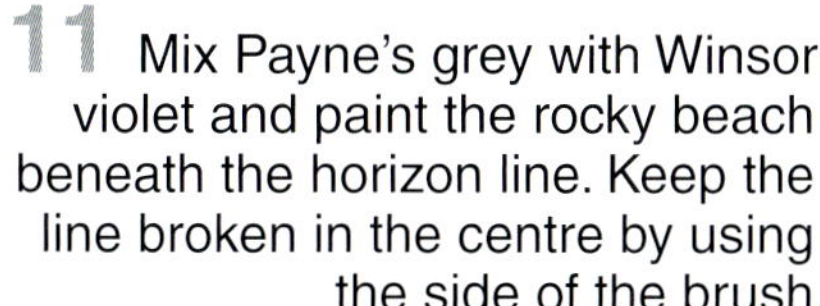

11 Mix Payne's grey with Winsor violet and paint the rocky beach beneath the horizon line. Keep the line broken in the centre by using the side of the brush.

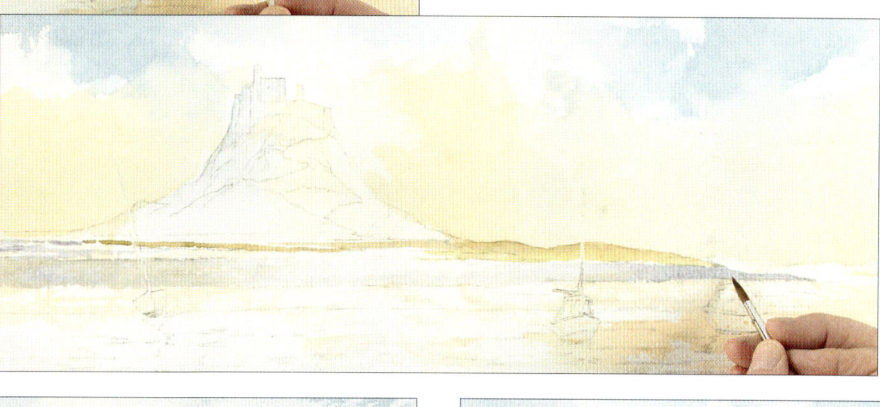

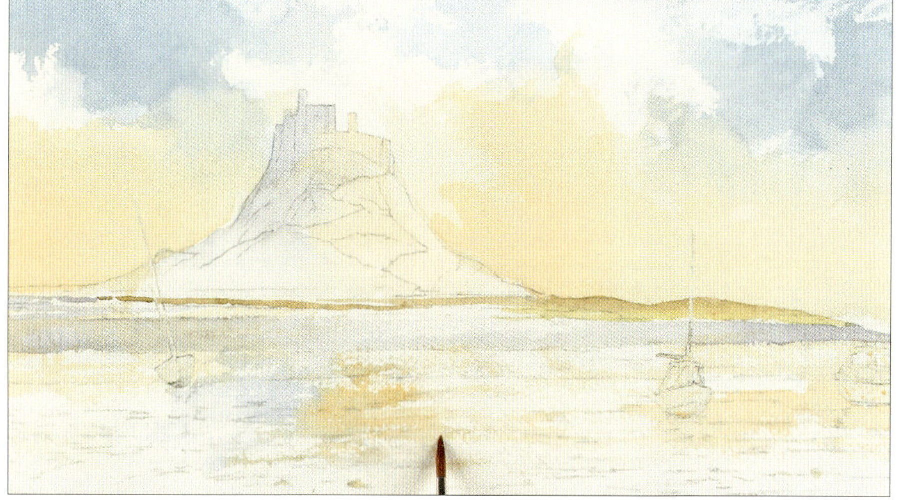

12 Pick up the reflections of the castle and hill in the water using a mix of Payne's grey, Winsor violet and cobalt blue. Use raw sienna to paint the reflections beneath the highlighted area.

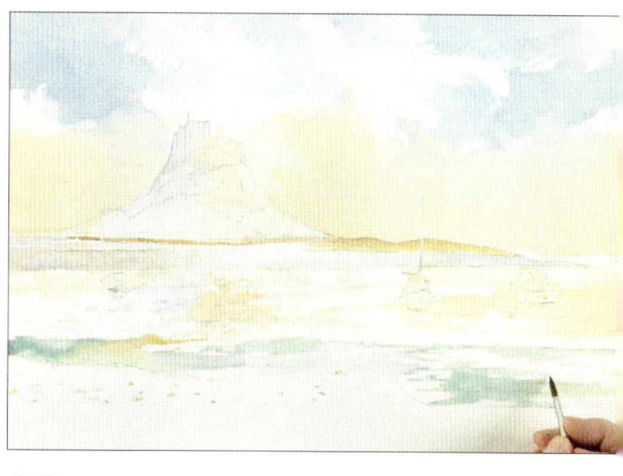

13 Still using the size 6 round, make a sea-green mix of cobalt blue and raw sienna, and pick out the green areas in the foreground. Vary the proportions of the colours in the mix and add touches of Payne's grey to create texture and interest.

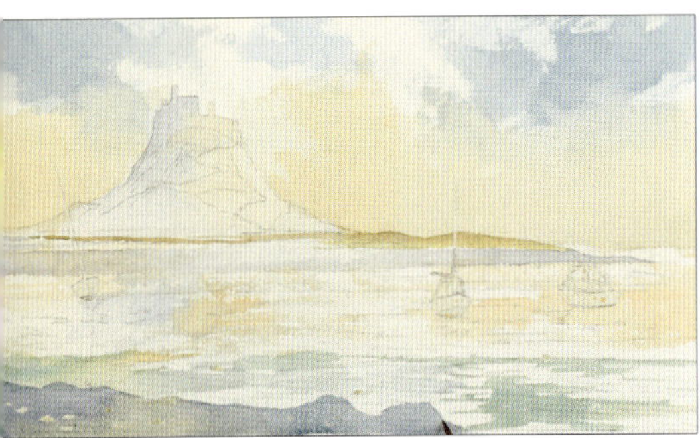

14 Add the dark area in the extreme foreground using Payne's grey, and add a little Winsor violet and raw sienna to achieve a variegated wash. Allow the paint to dry completely before continuing.

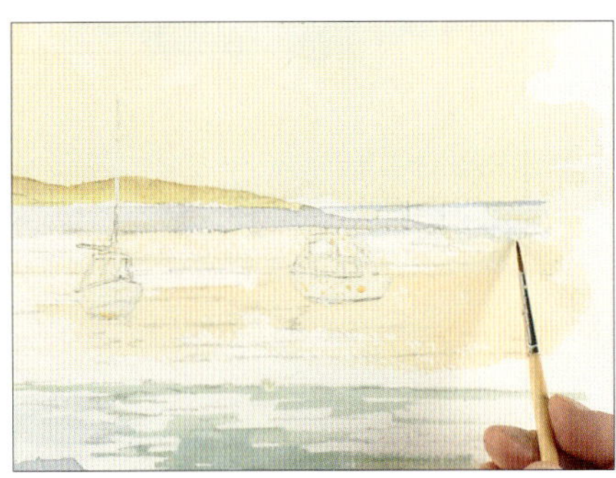

15 Use the size 2 round to draw a fine line of cobalt blue across the horizon on the right to establish the sea, then draw more dilute cobalt blue down beneath it.

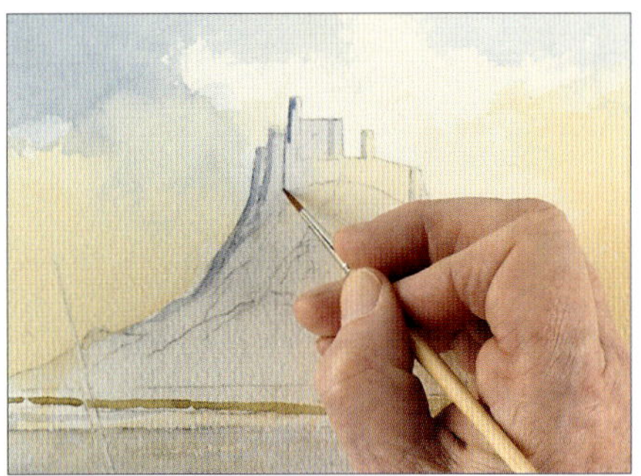

16 Still using the size 2 round, draw a dark mix of Payne's grey and cobalt blue down the left-hand sides of the towers.

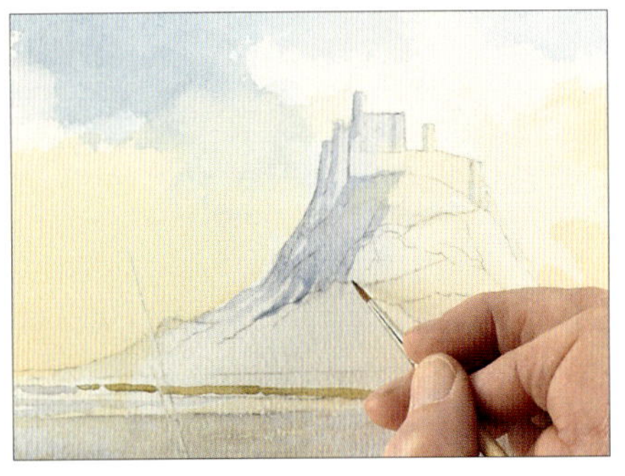

17 Use the same mix to shade the cliff on the shaded side.

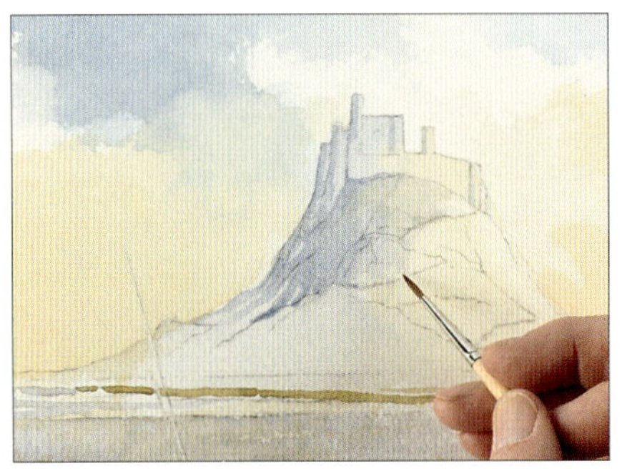

18 Draw the colour across the front of the cliff using a mix of Winsor violet and raw sienna.

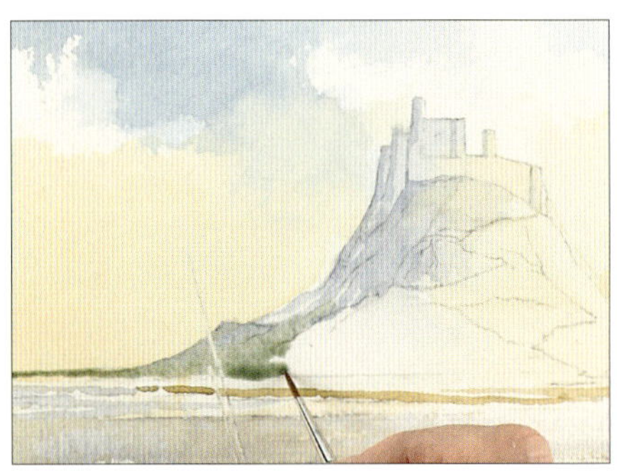

19 On the extreme left of the castle, apply a mix of Payne's grey and cobalt blue, then draw the green mix (French ultramarine and raw sienna) up on to the hill from the extreme left-hand horizon.

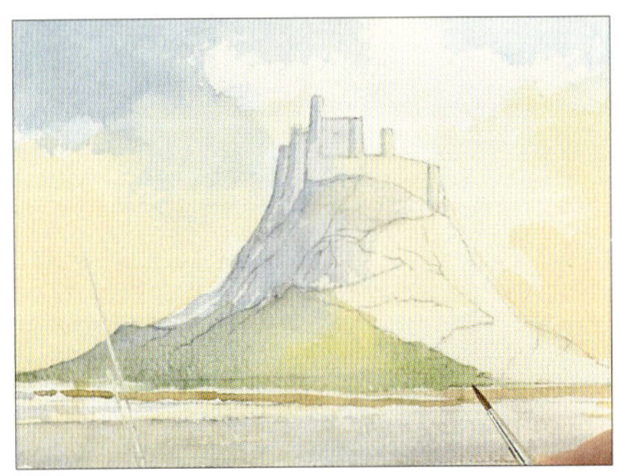

20 Continue drawing the green mix across the hill, adding Winsor yellow wet-in-wet where the light catches the front of the hillside.

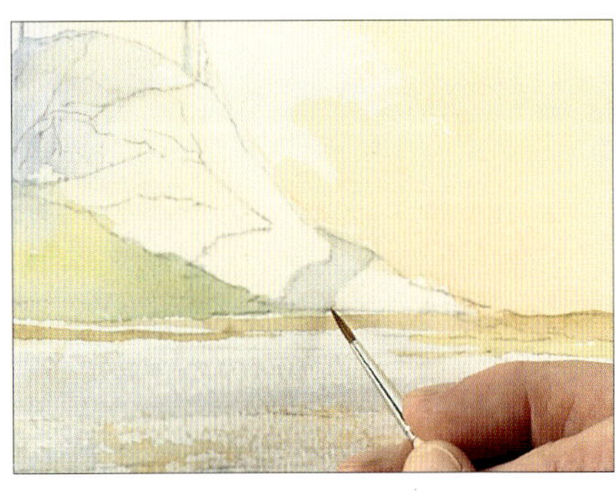

21 Paint in the roadway on the right of the hill using a mix of Payne's grey with a little Winsor violet added.

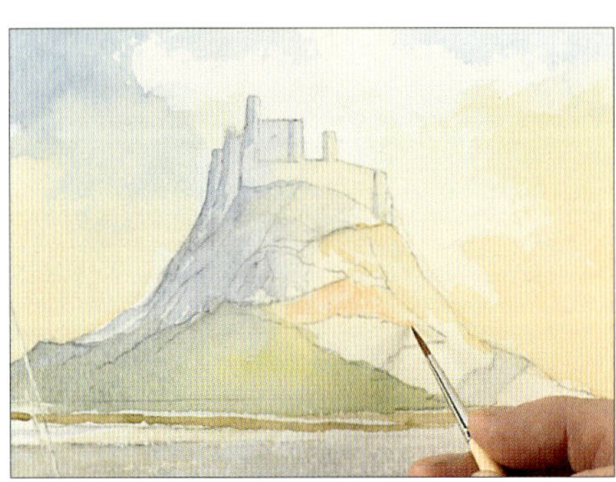

22 Pick up the lighter area of land beneath the castle using a sandy mix of Indian red and raw sienna, dropping in a mix of Indian red and Winsor yellow wet-in-wet.

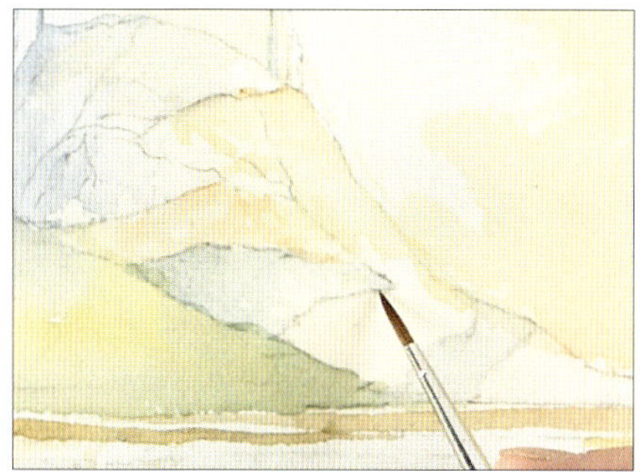

23 Mix Payne's grey with Winsor violet and paint in the section immediately beneath the sandy area.

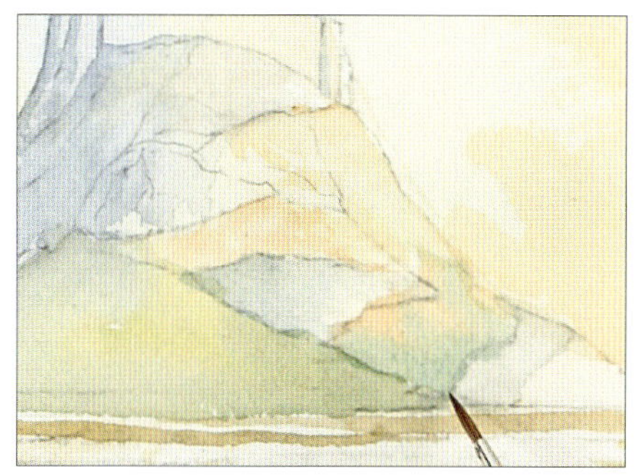

24 Paint the grassy area adjacent to the road with a fairly light wash of Indian red and Winsor yellow, adding a touch of viridian to vary the colour.

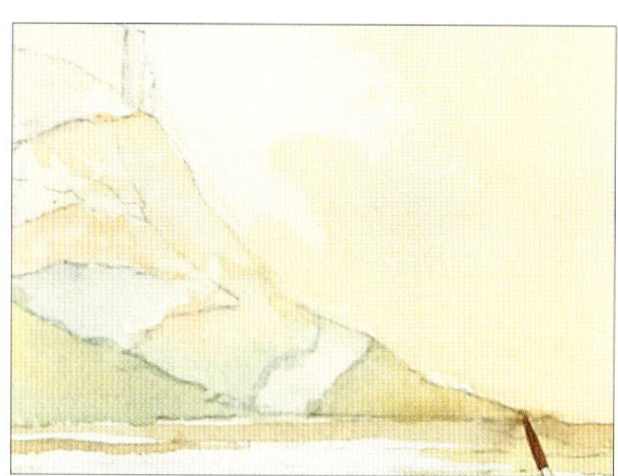

25 Using the green mix (French ultramarine and raw sienna), paint in the area to the right of the road to finish the hillside.

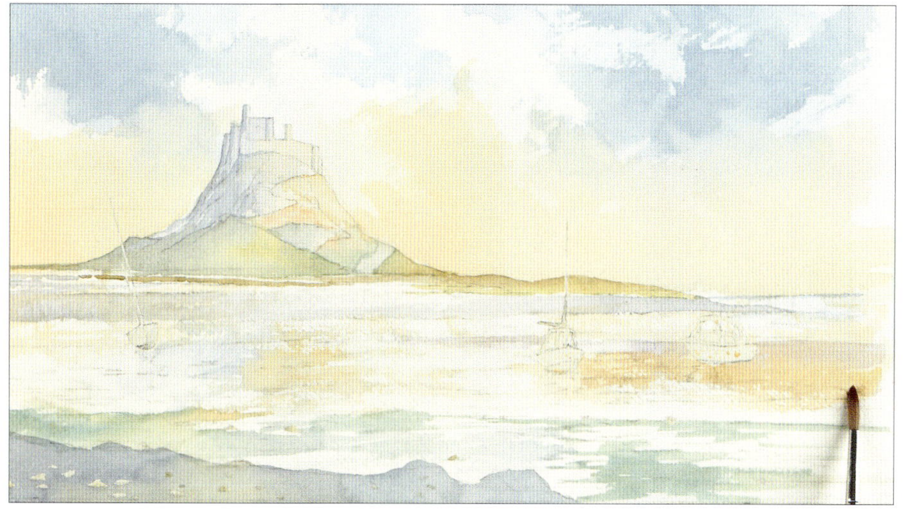

26 Prepare Winsor violet and raw sienna. Change to the size 8 round and draw strokes of Winsor violet over the midground on the right-hand side. Quickly change to the raw sienna and drag the side of the brush across the paper beneath the Winsor violet, blending the colour and creating a broken, glittering effect across the mudflat.

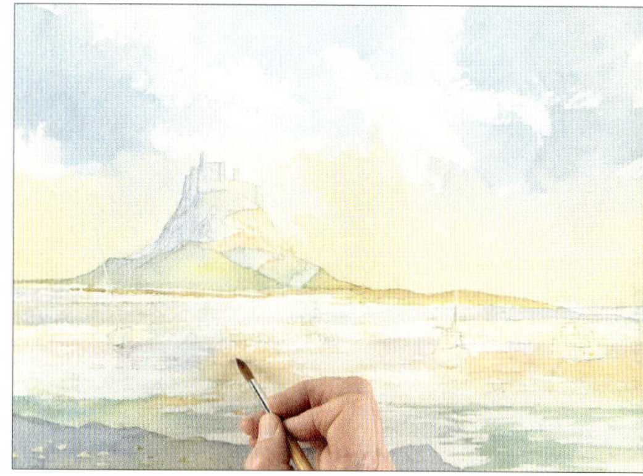

27 Make dilute mixes of Winsor violet with Indian red and drag the brush across the midground to suggest the mudbanks. Working wet-in-wet, draw raw sienna across beneath the mix to denote the wetter areas.

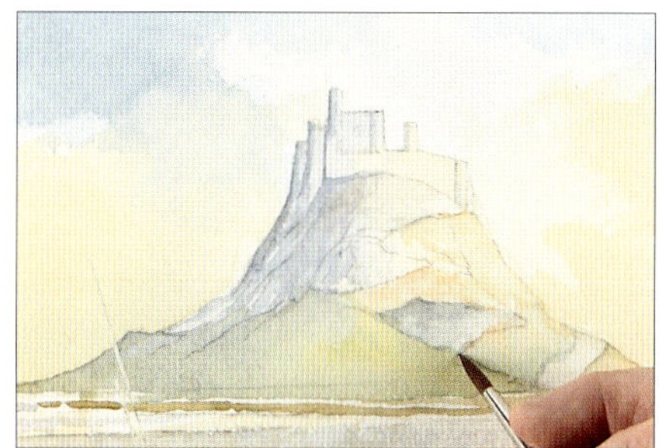

28 Reinforce the shadow areas on the castle using the tip of the size 6 round and Payne's grey with a hint of Winsor violet added. Warm the colour a little by adding a little Indian red wet-in-wet.

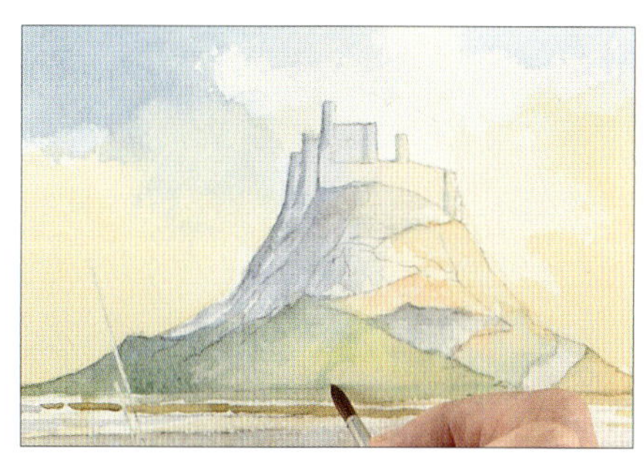

29 Mix some viridian with raw sienna and develop the left-hand side of the hill.

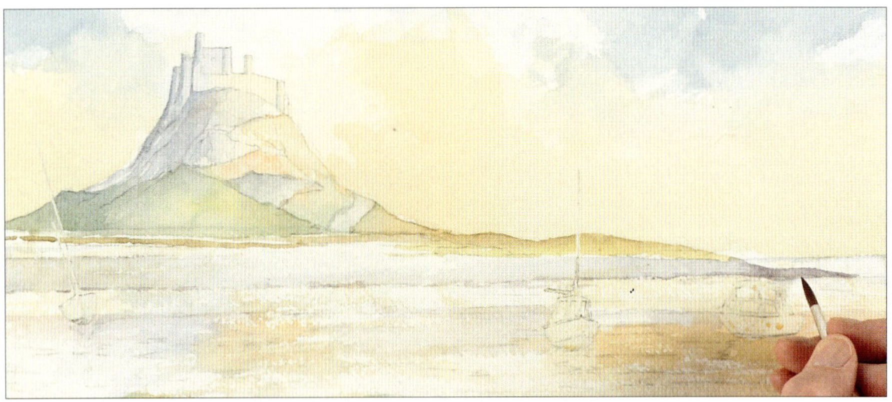

30 Make a dark mix of Indian red and Payne's grey and paint an irregular edge where the rocky beach meets the water.

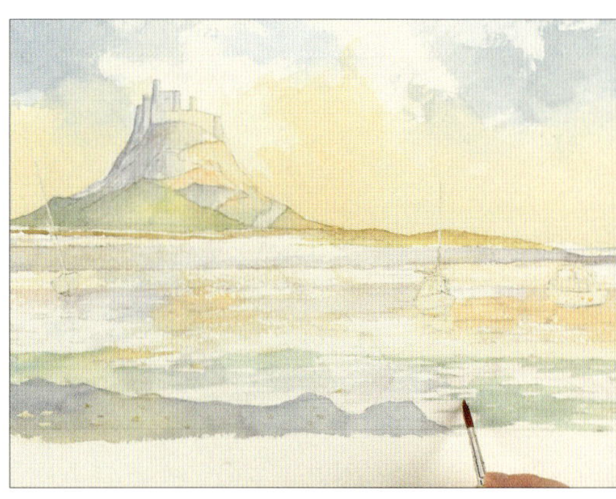

31 Drag a mix of Winsor violet and Indian red across the right-hand side of the foreground using the side of the size 6 round.

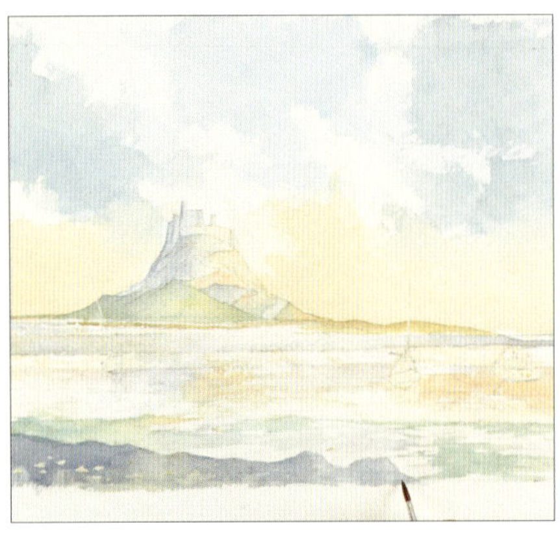

32 Suggest stronger structure in the dark area of the foreground using the tip of the size 6 with a dark mix of Payne's grey and Winsor violet.

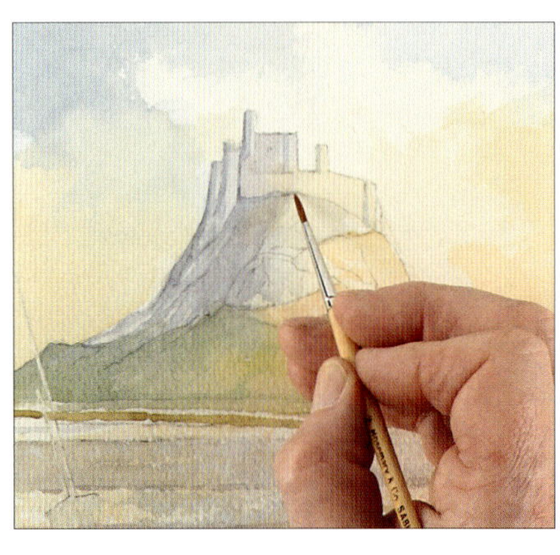

33 With a very dilute mix of Indian red and Payne's grey, use the size 2 round to add some midtones to the castle wall.

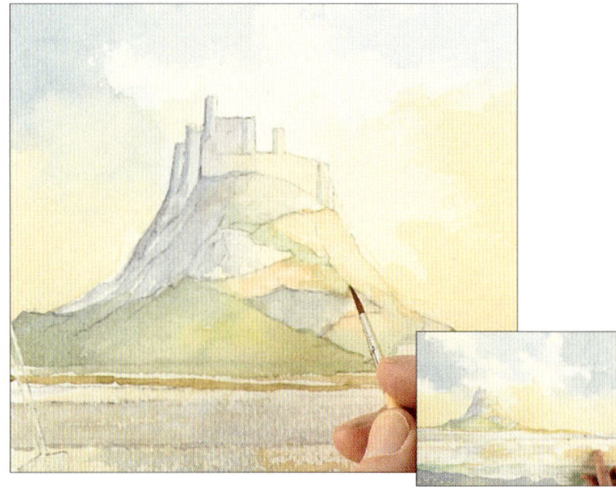

34 Use viridian with raw sienna to paint the grassy knoll near the road. Allow the painting to dry completely, then use a clean finger to remove the masking fluid (see inset).

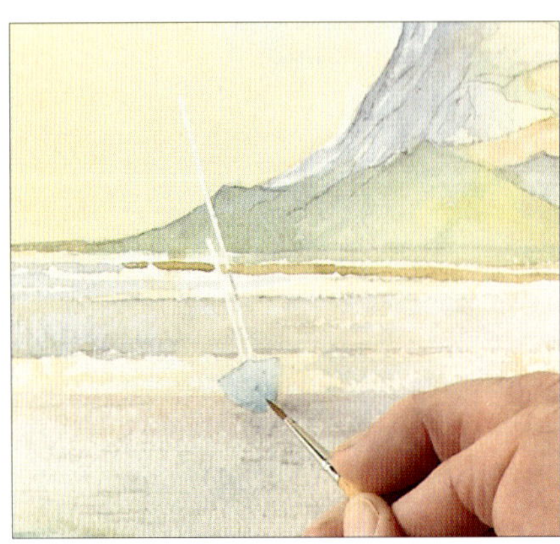

35 Using the size 2 round, paint the left-most boat with cerulean blue. Allow to dry.

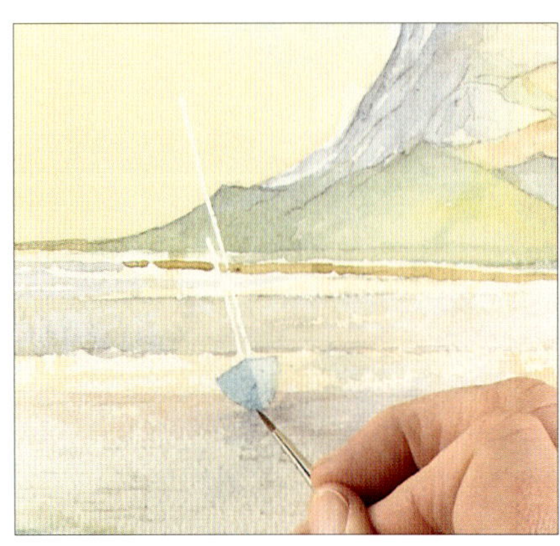

36 Glaze the left-hand side of the hull and add a subtle shadow beneath it, using cerulean blue.

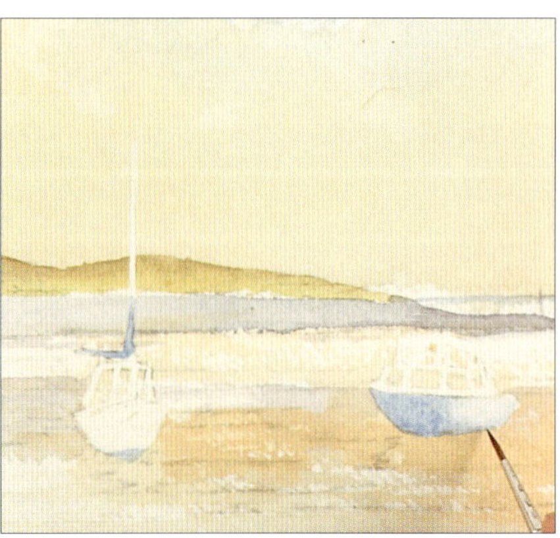

37 Paint the details of the middle boat's hull and the base of its mast with cobalt blue, then use the same colour to paint the right-most boat's hull, blending the colour out to the right to give it a highlight.

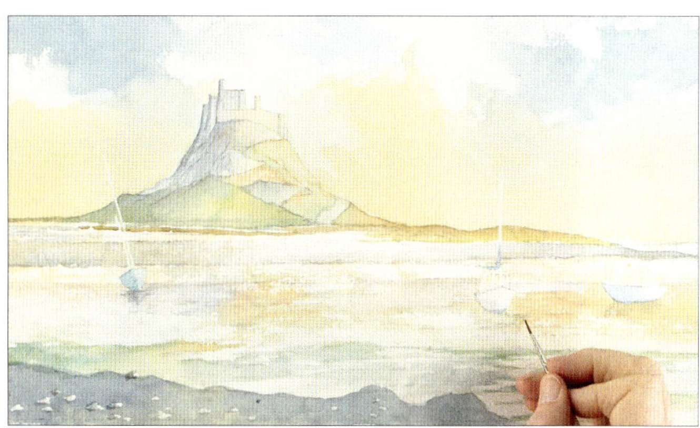

38 Using the same mix, add shadows to the left-hand sides and bases of the rocks in the foreground, and to add shadows beneath all of the boats using short zigzag strokes.

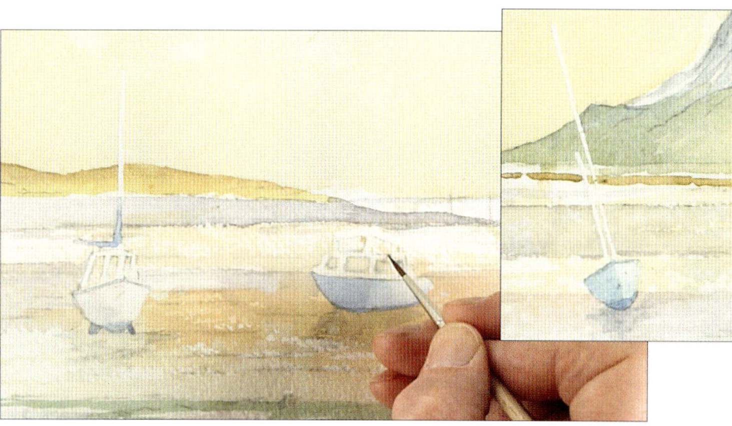

39 Use the tip of the size 1 round with dilute Payne's grey to add some details to the boats on the right-hand side, adding shadows to the edges of the windows, mooring struts and other details. Use the same colours to darken the details on the left-hand boat (see inset).

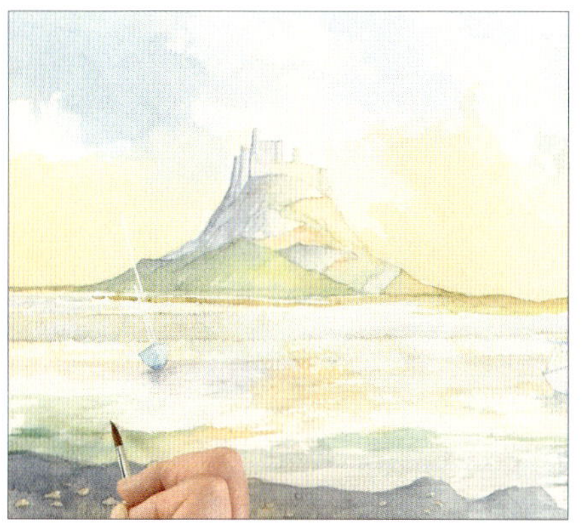

40 Switch to the size 6 round and strengthen the colours across the left-hand side of the painting, using glazes of dilute Payne's grey for the areas of shadow and background and viridian and Winsor yellow in the foreground.

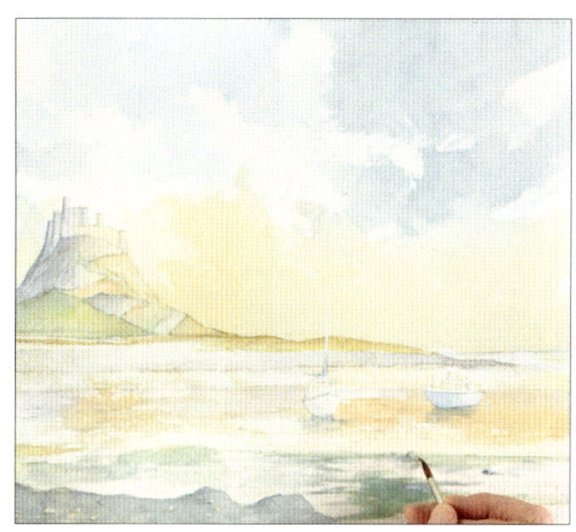

41 Break up the mudflat in the foreground with short, horizontal strokes of Payne's grey.

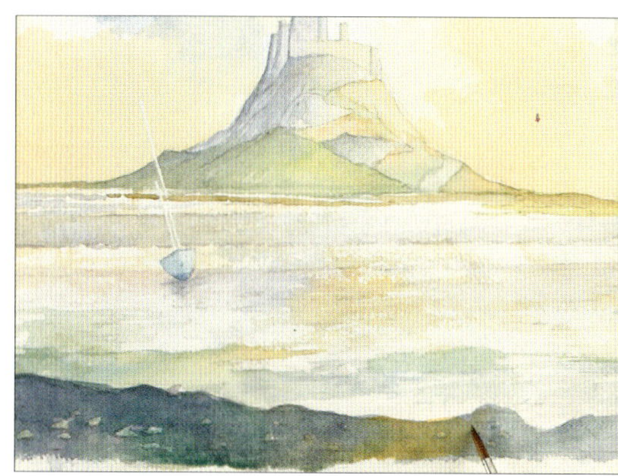

42 Still using the size 6 round, glaze some raw sienna over the foreground dark area, then drop in Payne's grey and viridian.

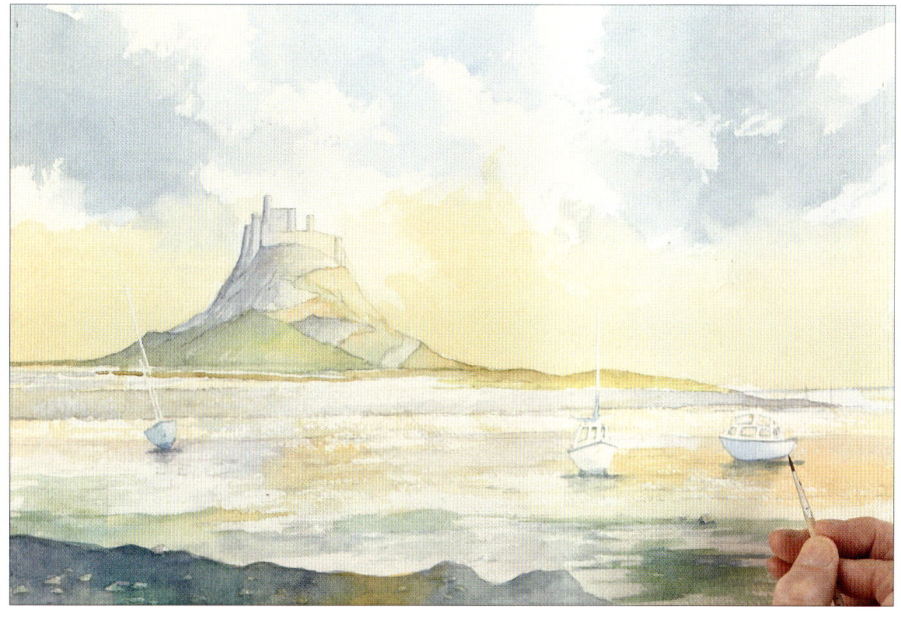

43 Reinforce the shadows beneath the boats with Payne's grey, then switch to the size 1 round and strengthen the shadows in the cabin windows to finish.

Overleaf
The finished painting.

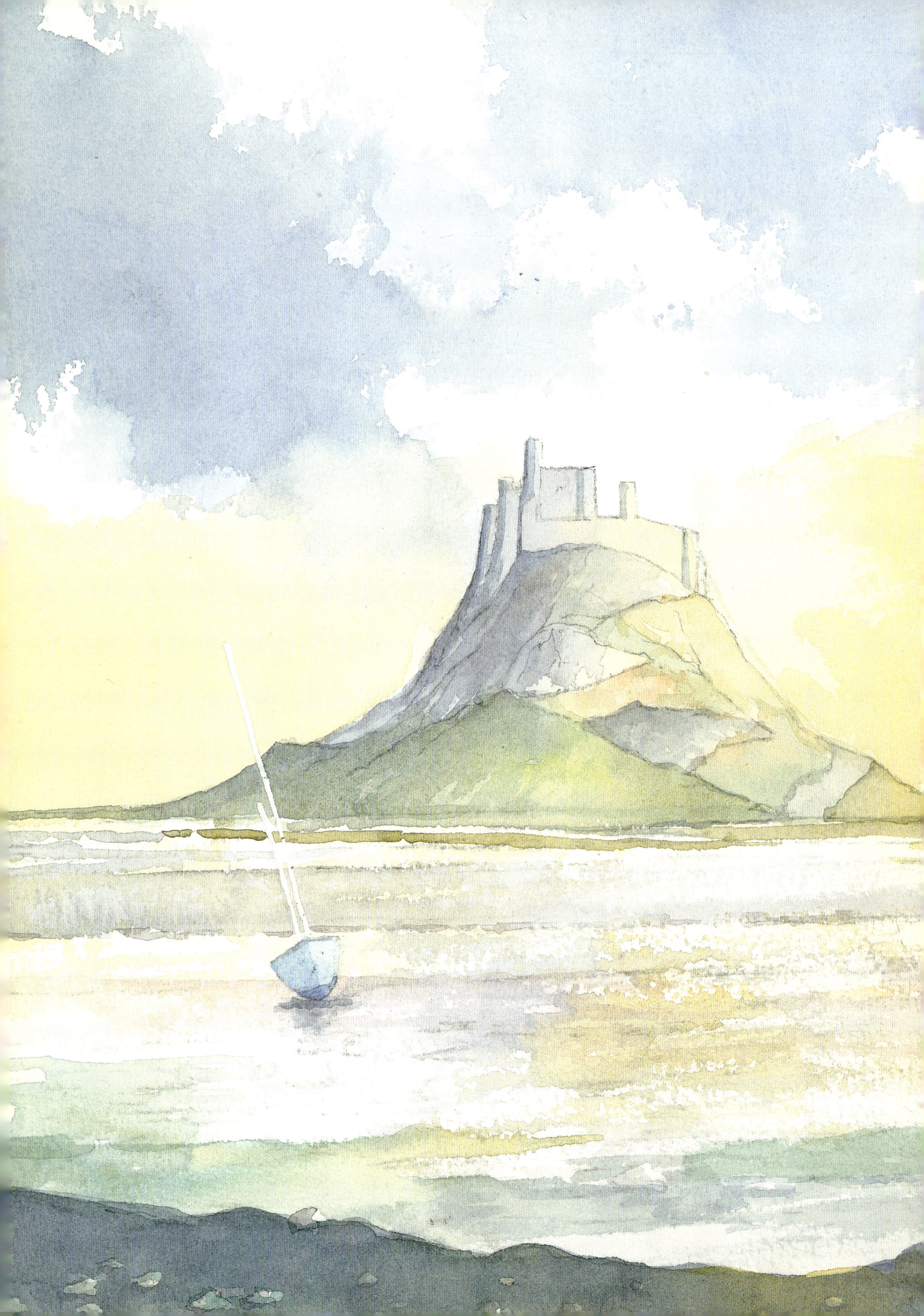

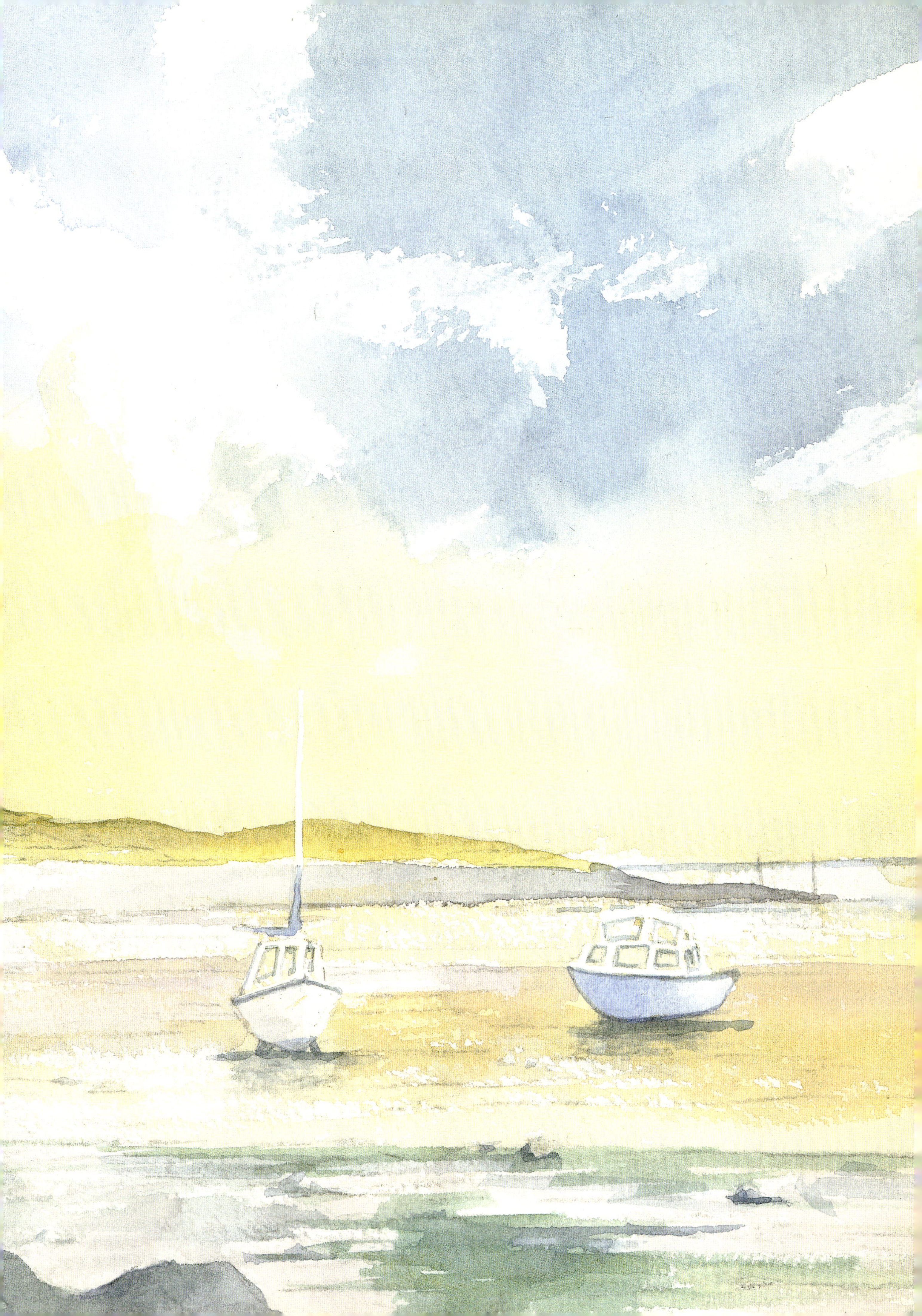

Marshland Windmill

TRACING 3

Coastlines often have many interesting areas for outdoor painting, even if the sea is not a major part of the composition. Cley Mill, which dominates the skyline for miles around the UK's Norfolk coast, is a perfect example. This viewpoint is taken from a path which runs between the mill and the sea. The marshlands separate the occasional flowers of the foreground from the background water inlet with the mill and surrounding houses. I have placed the mill on the area of the golden section so that the eye can go towards the mill, explore the houses and move down to the interesting foreground.

The light source in this painting is on the right, so apply darker colours and shadows on the left of objects.

You will need

Saunders Waterford Not 640gsm (300lb) watercolour paper, 56 x 38cm (22 x 15in)

Colours: cobalt blue, Payne's grey, Indian red, burnt umber, viridian, Winsor yellow, raw sienna and cadmium yellow

Brushes: size 16 round, size 14 round, size 6 round, size 10 round, size 4 round, size 2 round, size 8 round, size 1 round and 12mm (½in) Comber

White gouache

Masking tape and board

Masking fluid and old brush

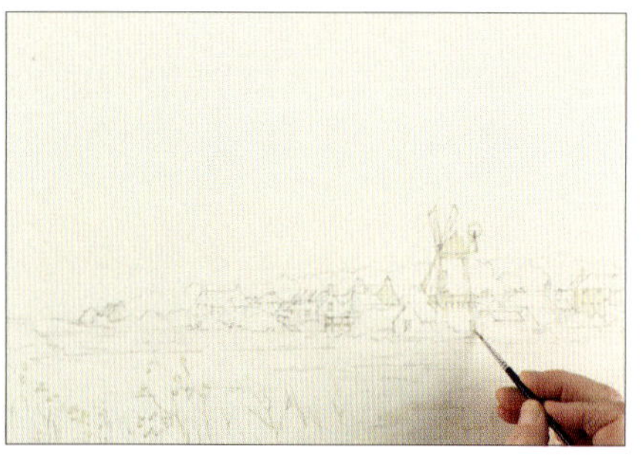

1 Following the instructions on page 9, transfer the tracing to your paper and run masking tape down the edges of the paper to secure it to the board. Using an old brush, apply masking fluid to the flowerheads, wetland and buildings, paying particular attention to the windmill itself.

2 Use the size 16 round to lay in a wash of cobalt blue on the sky, using clean water to diffuse it out as you work towards the horizon. Use light diagonal brushstrokes, and turn the brush as you work to get a loose, natural feel to the clouds.

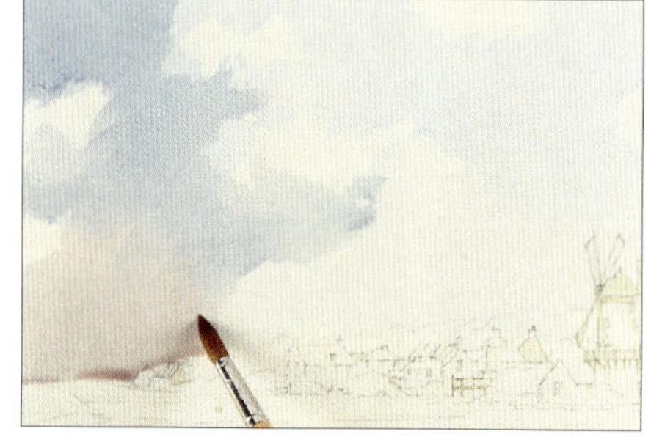

3 While the paint dries, change to the size 14 round and prepare a sky mix of Payne's grey and cobalt blue, and some pure Indian red. Apply the sky mix to the top left, and work downwards to the horizon, adding Indian red wet-in-wet at the bottom.

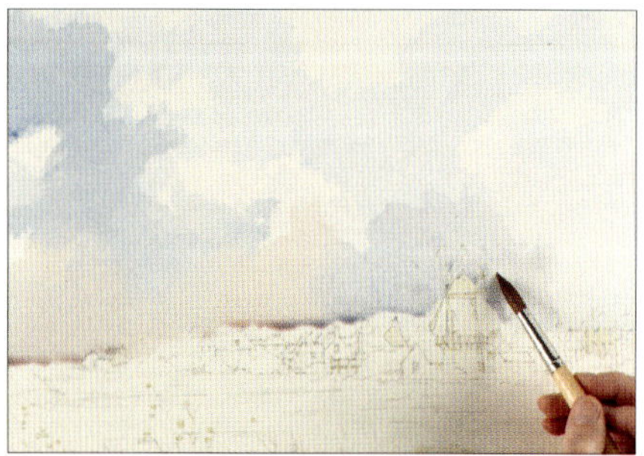

4 Continue working the sky mix and Indian red along the horizon line to the right, making the cloud bank behind the mill a little darker then the rest of the sky by working in more of the sky mix.

5 As you reach the right-hand side of the picture, work more Indian red on the horizon, then add progressively more sky mix as you work up to the top of the picture. Allow to dry thoroughly.

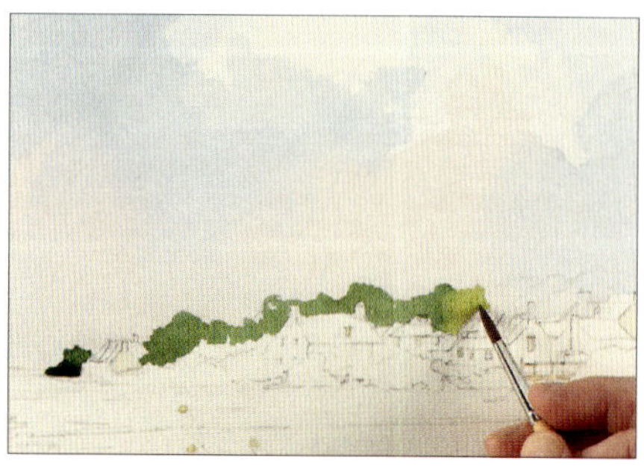

6 Starting from the left, use a size 6 round to paint in the background foliage using a dark green mix of burnt umber and viridian. Add touches of Winsor yellow to vary the hue.

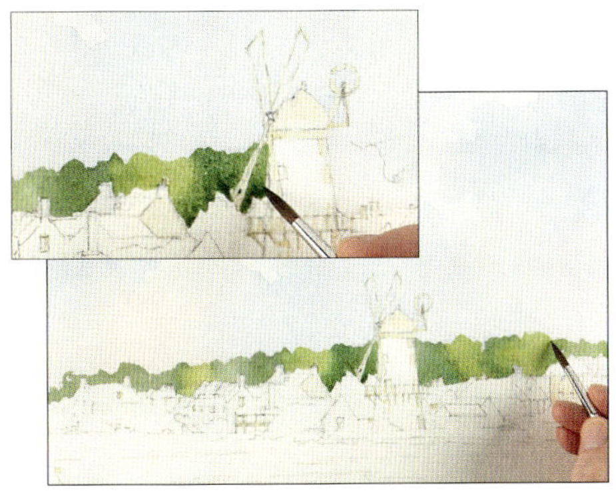

7 Using the same dark green mix, continue working to the right. Pay special attention when you come to the sails of the windmill, using the tip of the brush to pick the mill out from the background with negative painting (see inset), then continue working past the mill to the right-hand edge.

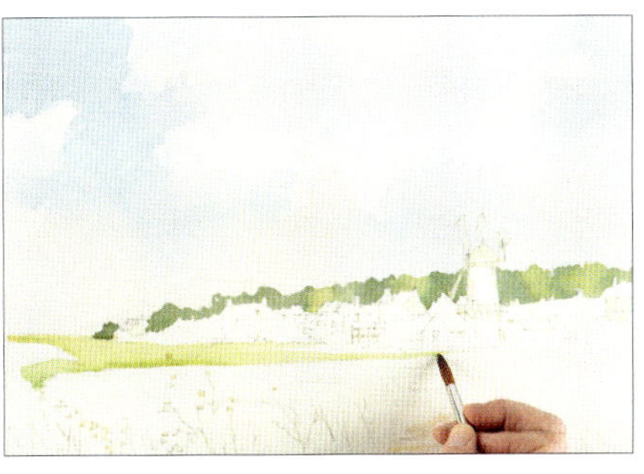

8 Make a mid-range mix of burnt umber, viridian and Winsor yellow. Starting from the left-hand side, use the size 10 round to paint this mid-range mix on to the marsh in front of the houses.

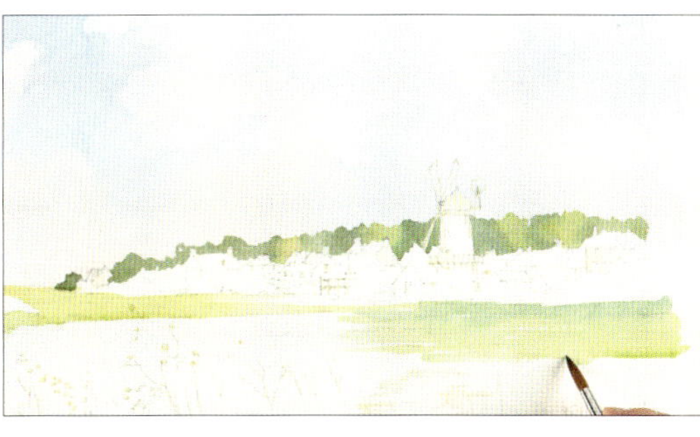

9 Using broad horizontal strokes, use the dark green mix to paint in from the right-hand side, adding Winsor yellow wet-in-wet as you advance from the horizon.

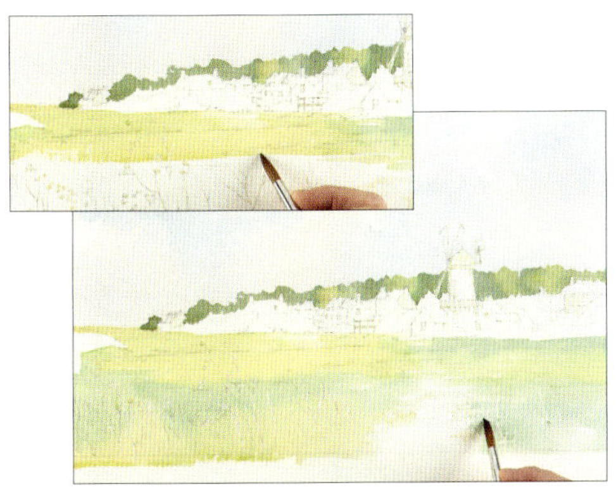

10 Create a sunlit effect by painting pure Winsor yellow wet-in-wet on the left-hand side (see inset), then paint the rest of the foreground using the washes you have prepared. Be sure to keep the wetland area that leads to the mill clean, as shown.

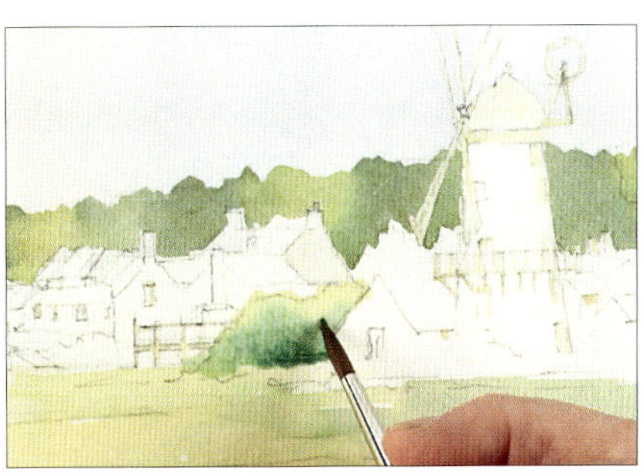

11 Using the dark green mix (burnt umber and viridian) with the size 6, paint the central trees in front of the houses. They need to be more detailed than the trees in the background, so add Winsor yellow as a highlight at the top.

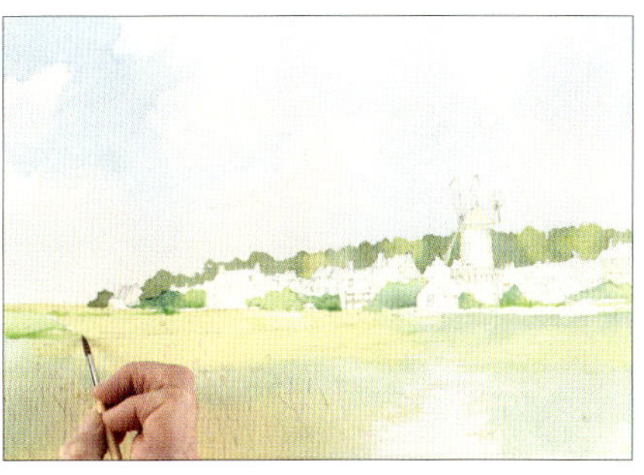

12 Paint the rest of the midground foliage in the same way, then use the mid-range mix (burnt umber, viridian and Winsor yellow) to paint in the white area on the upper left.

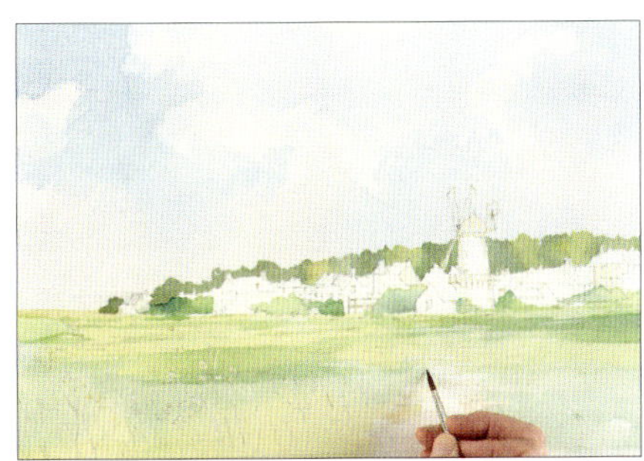

13 Return to the foreground, painting bold horizontal strokes wet-on-dry across the marshland using the mid-range mix and the dark green mix.

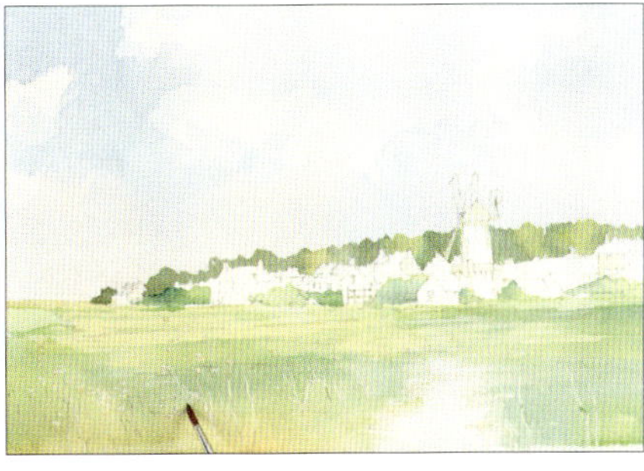

14 Work to the bottom of the painting, varying the combination of the mixes. Add pure raw sienna on the area to the lower left.

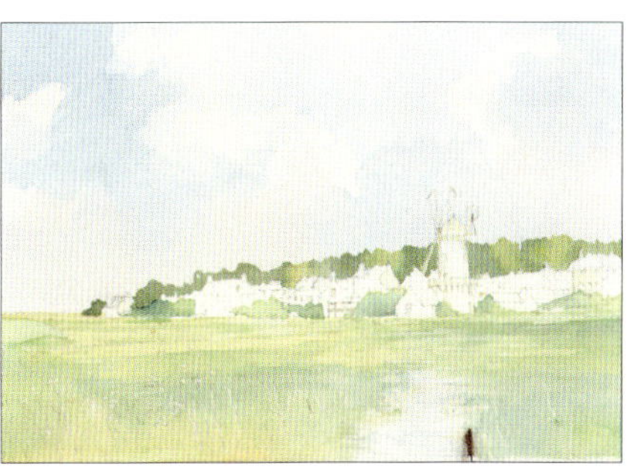

15 Use the side of the size 6 brush to drag cobalt blue across the wetland area at the front, giving a fresh, sparkling quality.

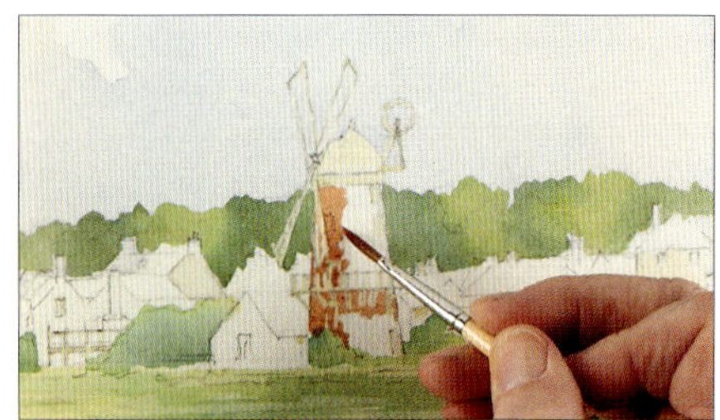

16 Prepare a mix of Indian red and a little raw sienna and change to the size 4 round to paint the shaded side of the windmill.

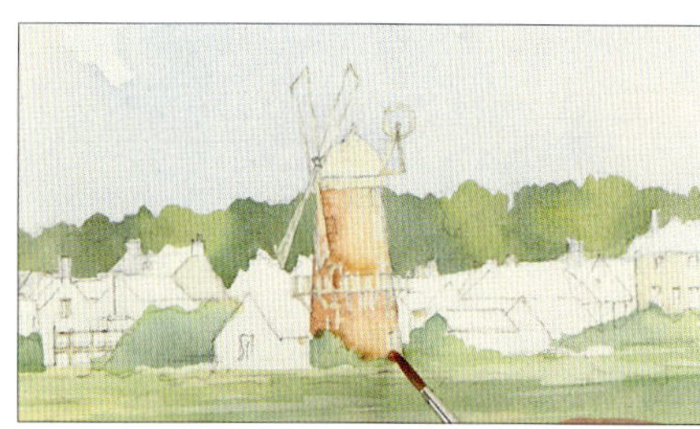

17 Working wet-in-wet, add more raw sienna to the mix and paint the highlighted part of the mill on the right-hand side.

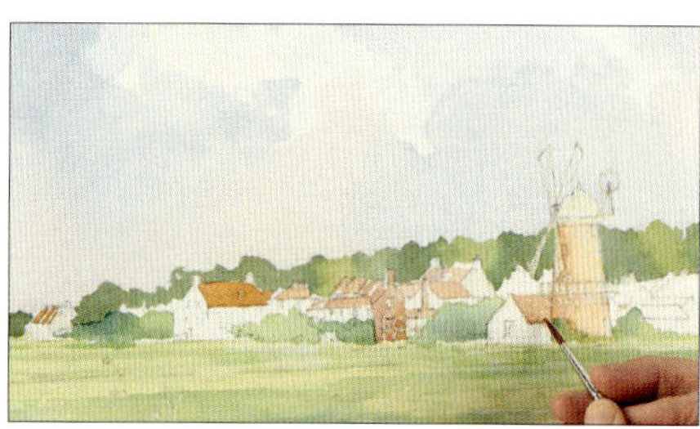

18 Paint in parts of the buildings on the far left, using mixes of Indian red and a cadmium yellow in varying proportions.

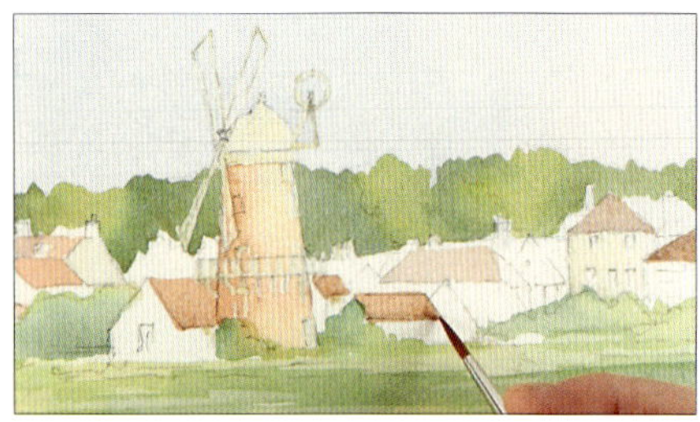

19 Still varying the proportions of the colours, paint parts of the buildings on the right. Add Payne's grey to the mix for further variation.

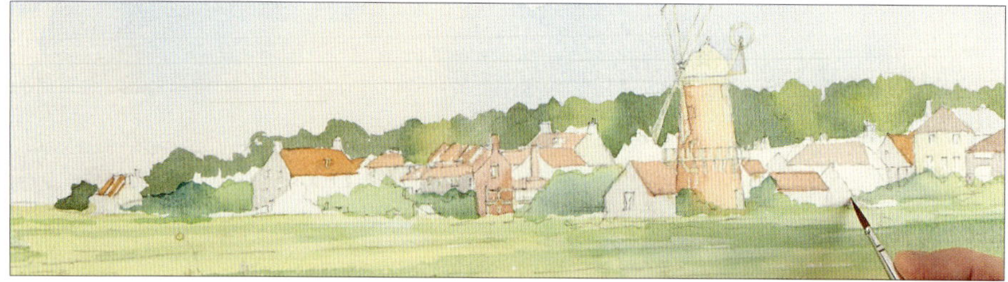

20 Make a rich, dilute grey from Payne's grey, cobalt blue and a little Indian red, and use this to further develop the buildings.

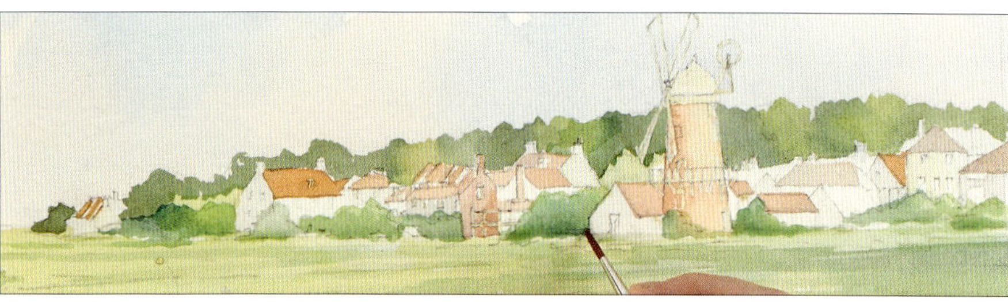

21 Using the tip of the size 4 round and the dark green mix (burnt umber and viridian), pick out details and differentiate the trees in the background from each other. Use the same mix to add in any midground bushes and trees that you may have missed.

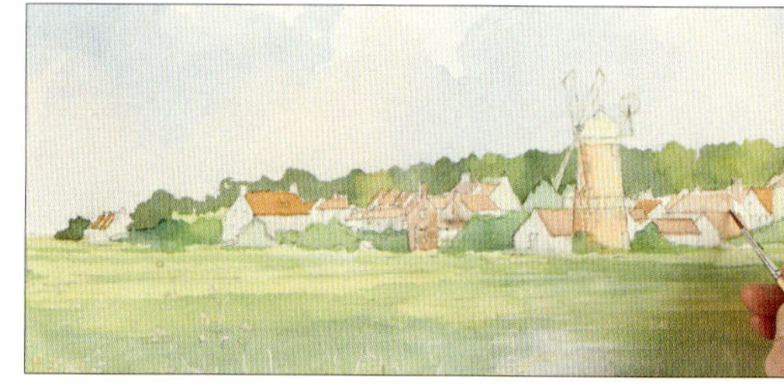

22 Use the Indian red and raw sienna mix with the size 2 brush to put in any last touches on the buildings for this first wash.

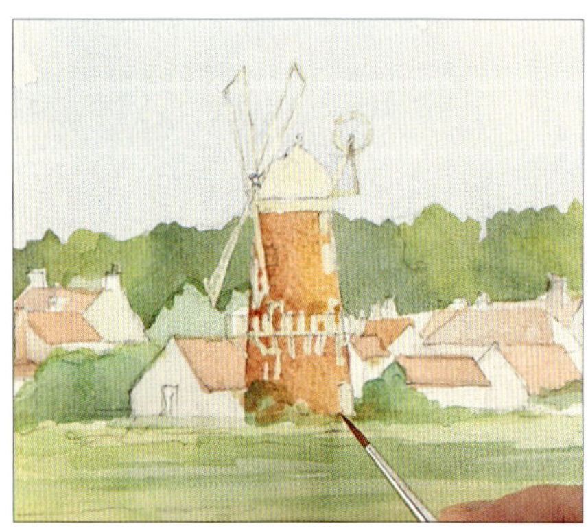

23 Strengthen the mill with the same mix, using more Indian red on the shaded side and more raw sienna on the lighter side.

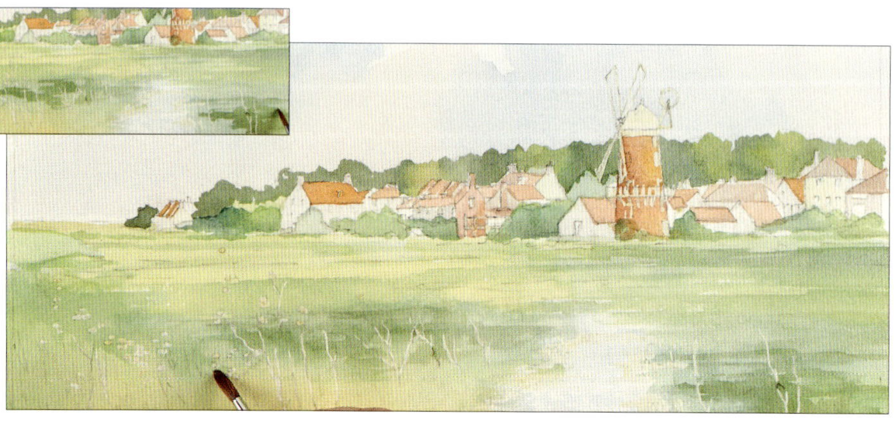

24 Using loose horizontal strokes of the size 8 brush, apply a glaze of the dark green mix to areas of the foreground to add interest (see inset). Use clean water to diffuse the paint to avoid hard edges.

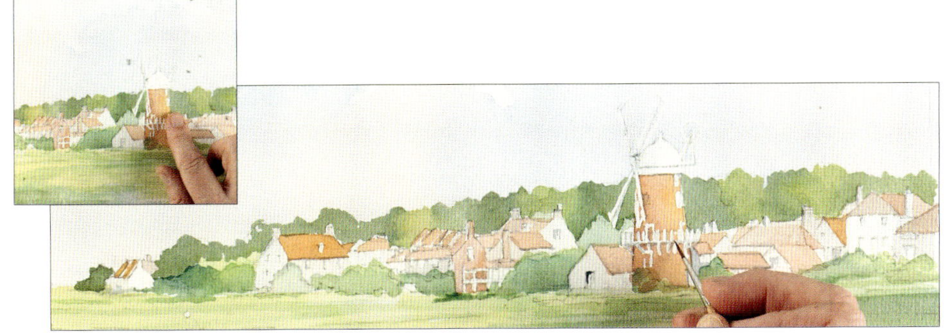

25 Allow the painting to dry, then use a clean finger to remove all of the masking fluid (see inset). Using the size 1 round and Payne's grey, paint in strategic details on the midground, such as windows and shadows beneath ledges and on the left-hand side of the chimneys. Pay particular attention to the mill, painting the shadows beneath the walkway and on the sails.

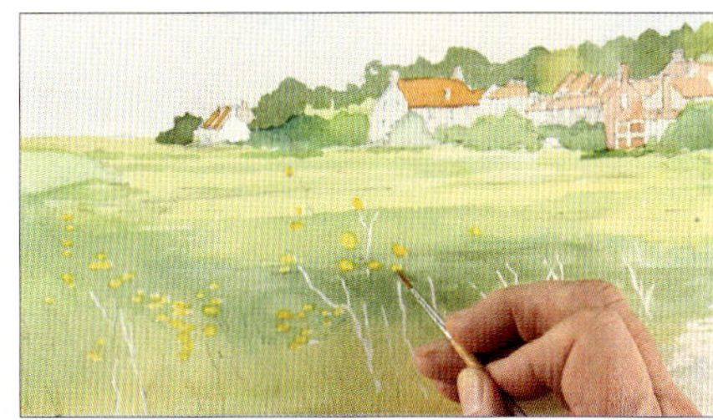

26 Make a bright yellow mix of Winsor yellow and cadmium yellow. Dot in the marsh flowers with the size 1 round in the left-hand side of the foreground.

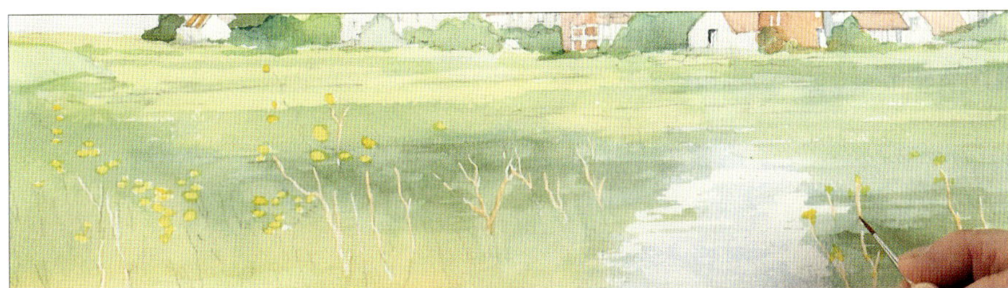

27 Dot in the flowers on the right-hand side, then use a mix of raw sienna with a hint of Indian red to paint all of the flower stems.

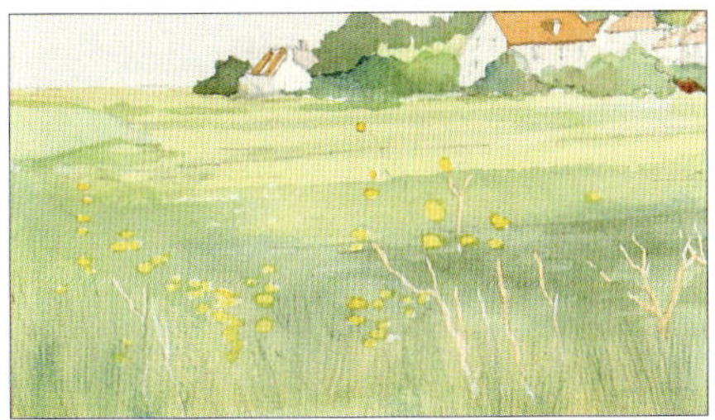

28 Change to the Comber brush, and draw a mix of viridian with a little burnt umber upwards from the bottom of the page, using light, vertical strokes. This creates a convincing effect of grasses and reeds in the foreground.

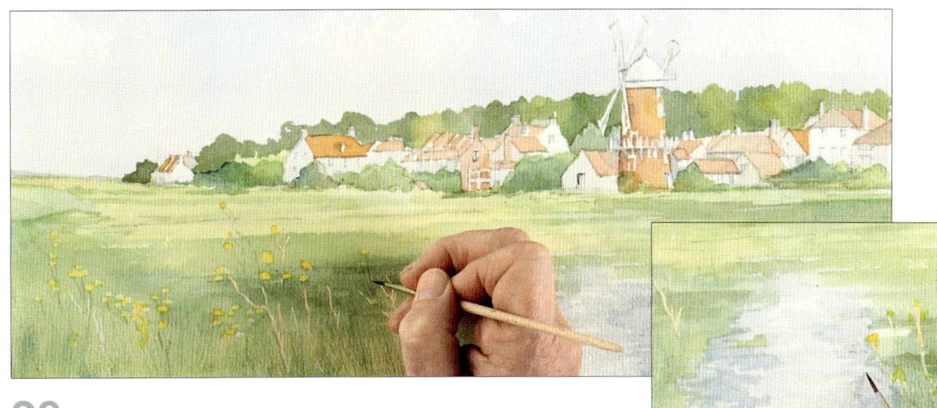

29 Change back to the size 1 brush and use a mix of cobalt blue and Payne's grey to strengthen the shadows on the chimneys, mill sails and on the edges of the wetland area (see inset).

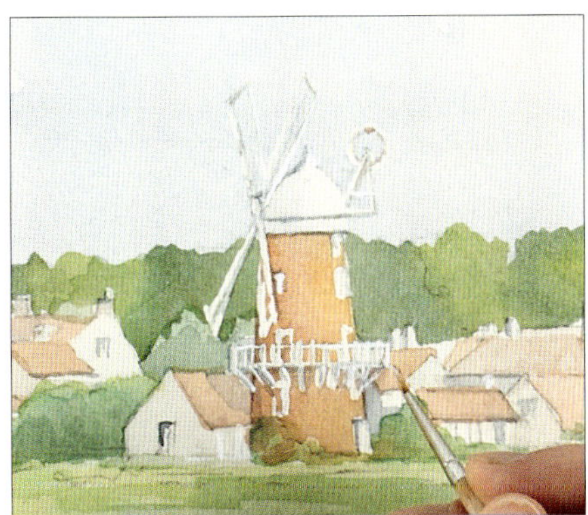

30 Use the size 1 to apply white gouache, very sparingly, to define the windows and mill sails.

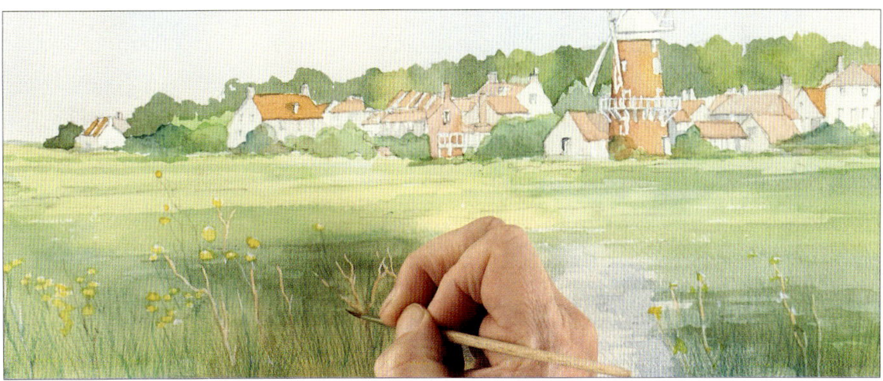

31 Finally, add some further darker grasses in the foreground with a dark green mix of viridian and burnt umber.

Overleaf

The finished painting.

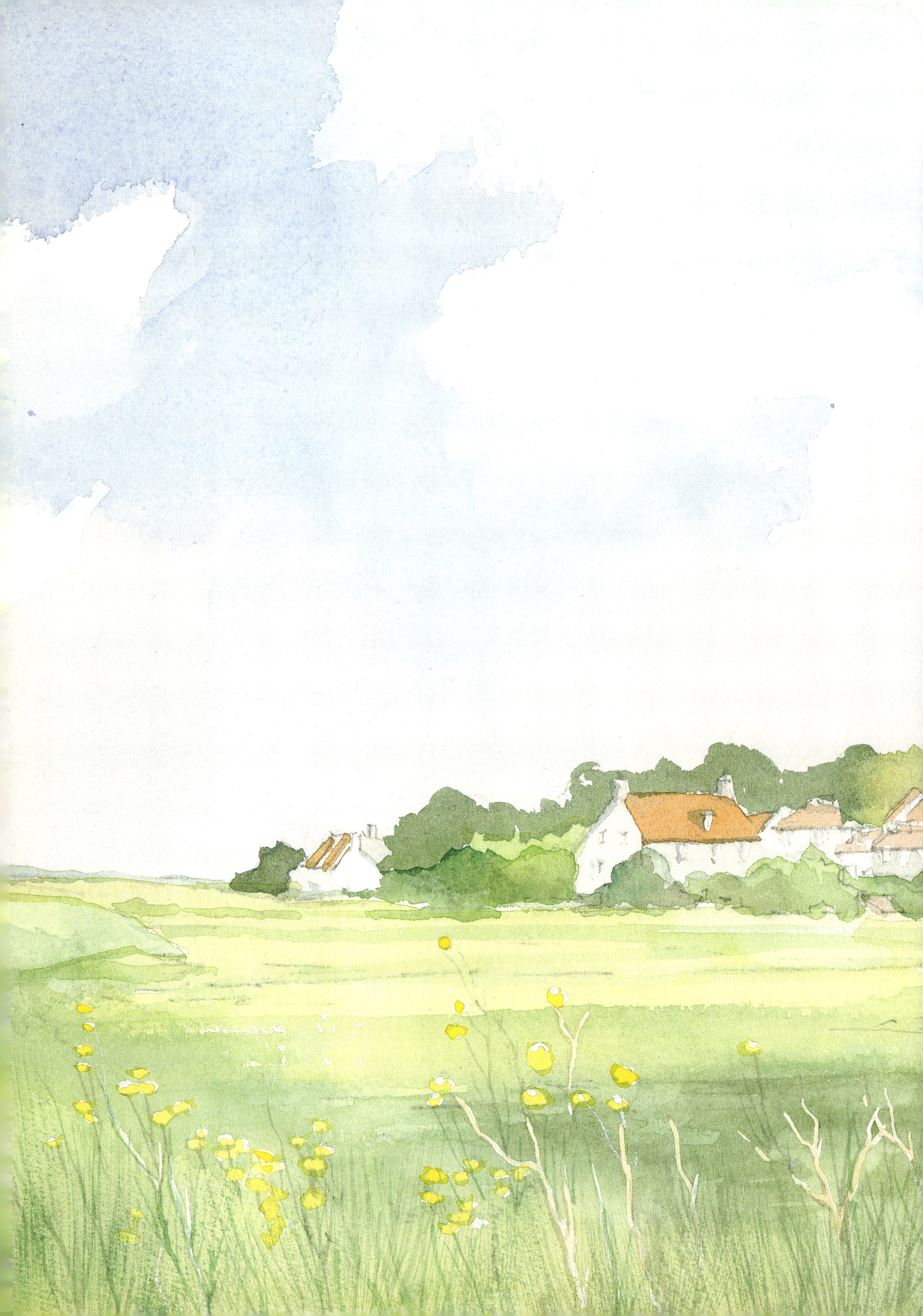

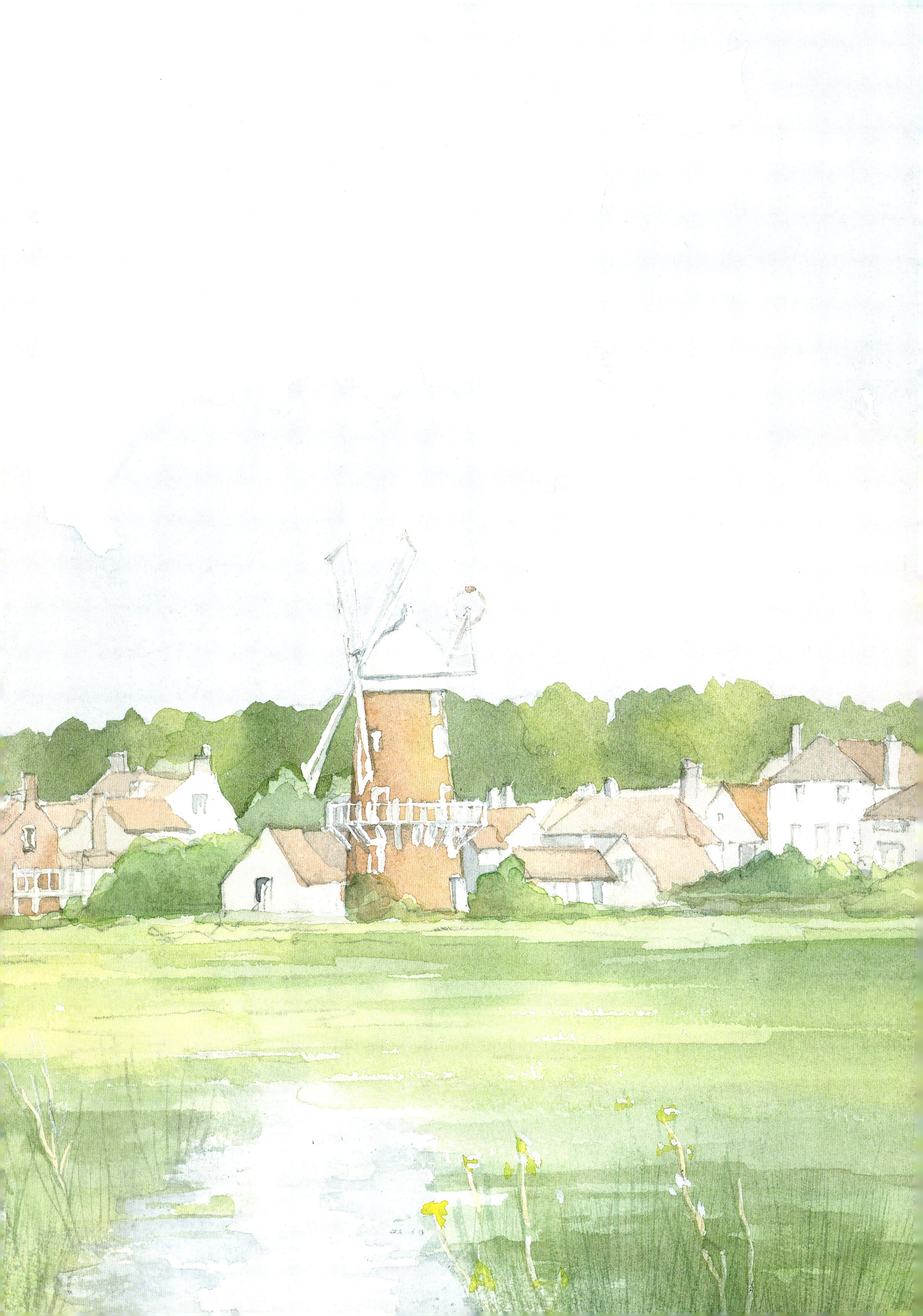

Coastal Cliffs

TRACING 4

Robin Hood's Bay, in the UK, lies between steep sandstone cliffs. This view is from the beach, looking inland. The central cliff captures the whole atmosphere of the village.

You will need

Saunders Waterford Not 640gsm (300lb) watercolour paper, 56 x 38cm (22 x 15in)

Colours: cobalt blue, raw sienna, Winsor yellow, Indian red, burnt umber, viridian, Payne's grey, cadmium red, cadmium yellow and Winsor green

Brushes: size 14 round, size 6 round, size 4 round, size 2 round and size 1 round

Masking tape and board

Masking fluid and old brush

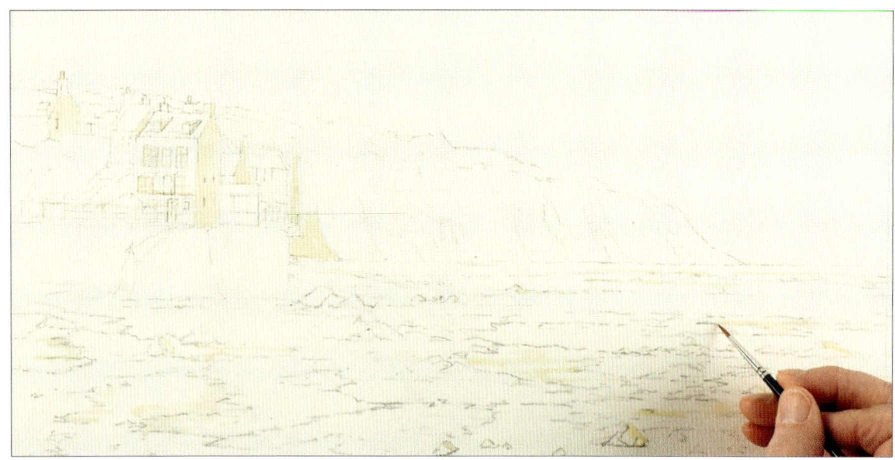

1 Following the instructions on page 9, transfer the tracing to your paper, then secure your paper to the board with masking tape at the edges. Apply masking fluid with an old brush to selected rocks and reflections in the rock pools in the foreground, the window frames in the midground, and the right-hand sides of some of the buildings.

Tip

The light is coming from the right, so masking fluid should be concentrated on this side of objects to preserve the highlights.

2 Prepare wells of cobalt blue and raw sienna. Use the size 14 round to lay in a wash of cobalt blue on the top half of the sky. Hold the brush at a diagonal to the horizon, and use loose strokes to leave clean white spaces as clouds, rotating the brush as you work to release the pigment.

3 Working wet-in-wet, apply raw sienna to the lower half of the sky down to the horizon.

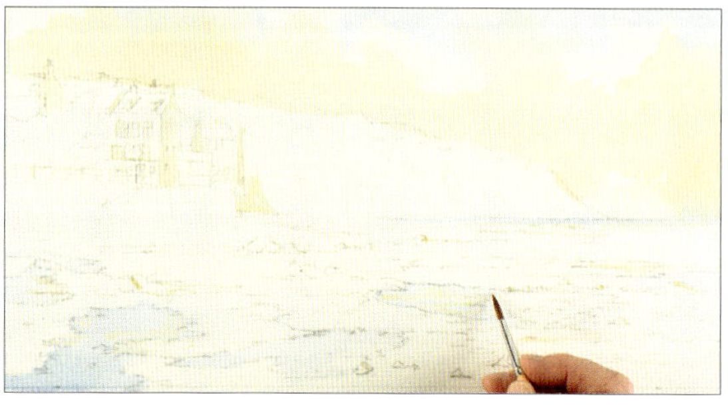

4 Using the tip of the size 6 round, fill in the rock pools and the sea at the horizon line with cobalt blue, dropping raw sienna in to the pools nearer the middle of the page, since these are reflecting the lower part of the sky. Allow to dry.

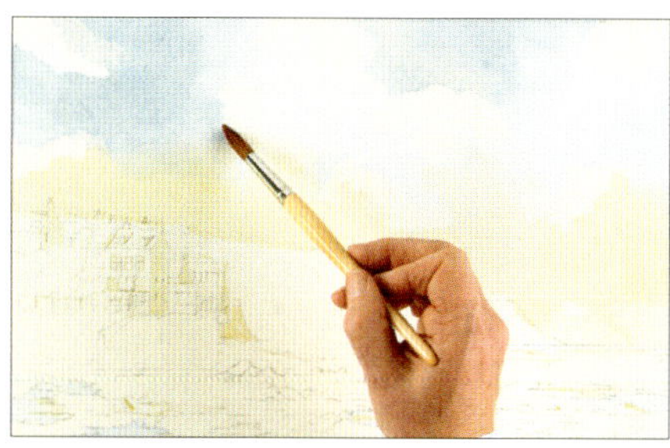

5 With the size 14 round and a dilute mix of Payne's grey and cobalt blue, lay in some darker areas next to the clouds to add some interest to the sky. Allow the paint to dry.

6 Paint in the grass at the top of the cliff with raw sienna and Winsor yellow wet-in-wet, using the size 4 round to work carefully around the buildings.

7 Lay a wash of raw sienna and a hint of Indian red into the cliffs themselves. Allow to dry, then bring out some initial details with dilute Indian red.

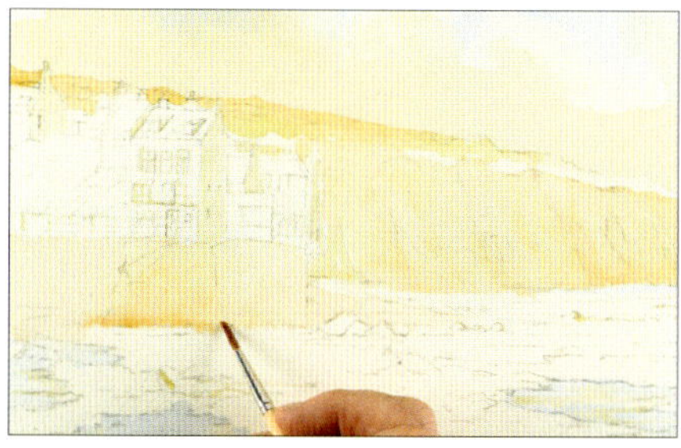

8 Continue to the left, using more raw sienna to paint the underside of the causeway and the area beneath the houses, again adding Indian red to add some variation at the base.

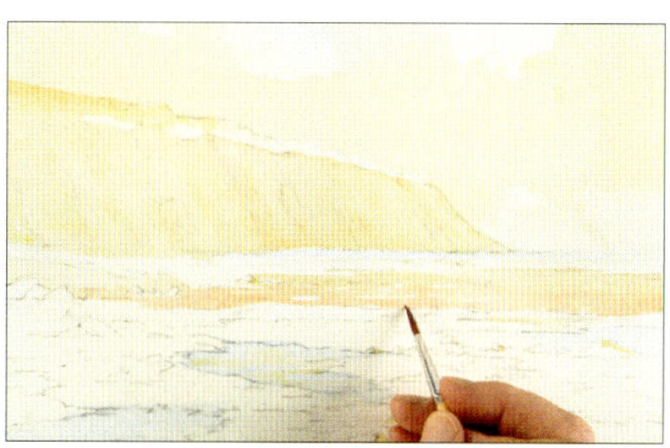

9 Use a wash of raw sienna and Indian red to paint around the sandy area and rock pools in the midground. Vary the proportions of the colours used to achieve a variegated appearance.

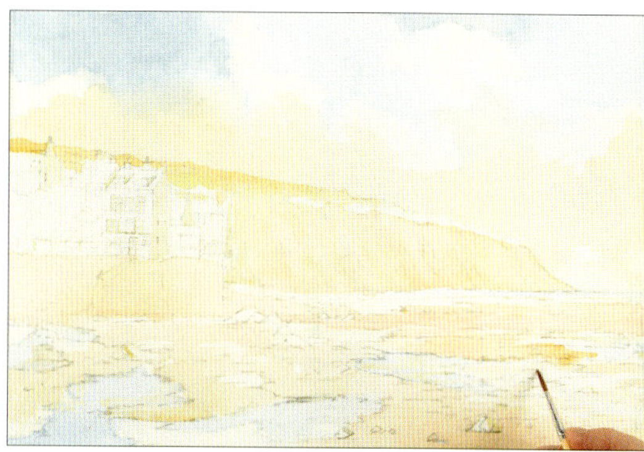

10 As you advance, use loose strokes with the same subtly varied colours to fill in the foreground to finish the initial washes. Allow the paint to dry thoroughly.

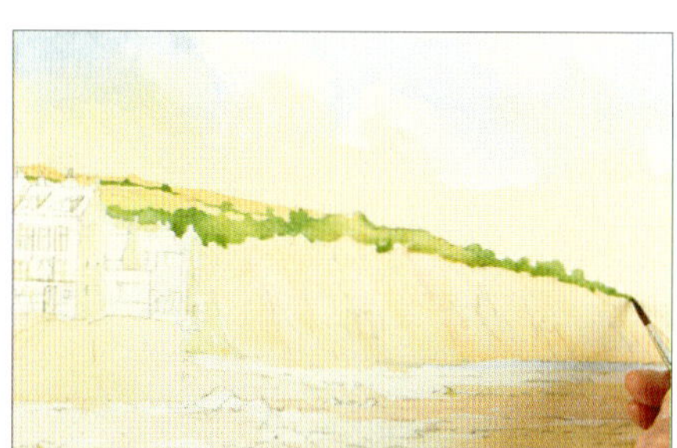

11 Paint the background foliage with the size 4 round and a dark green mix of burnt umber and viridian, varying the mix with an occasional touch of Winsor yellow.

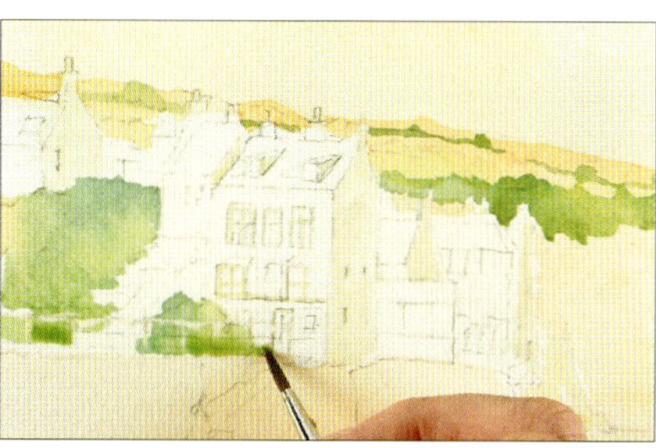

12 Starting with some raw sienna and adding touches of the dark green mix and Winsor yellow, lay in an initial wash on the foliage above the sea wall and on the bush in front of the main house on the left.

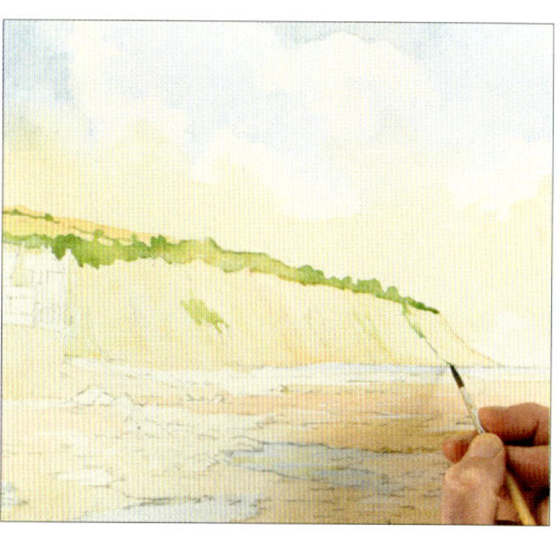

13 Use the same colours to add some touches of greenery to the cliff faces themselves.

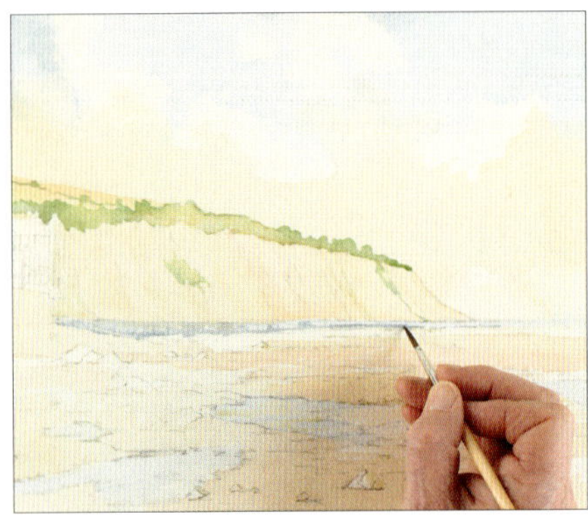

14 Still using the size 4 round, reinforce the sea below the cliffs with a strong line of the Payne's grey and cobalt blue mix, leaving small gaps. Add Payne's grey wet-in-wet at the base of the line.

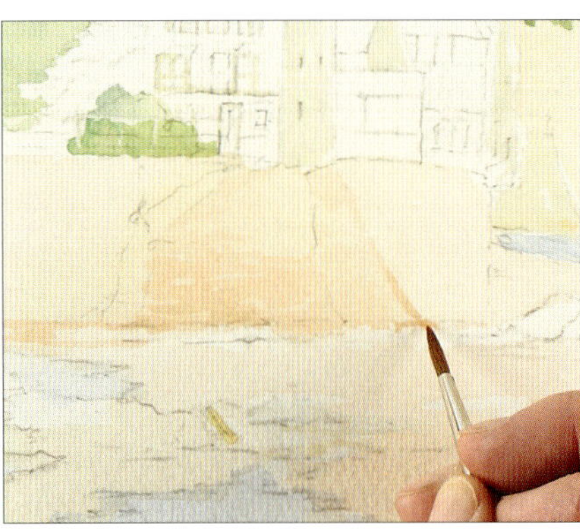

15 Paint subtle horizontal strokes of dilute Indian red with a little raw sienna to suggest brickwork on the sea wall as shown.

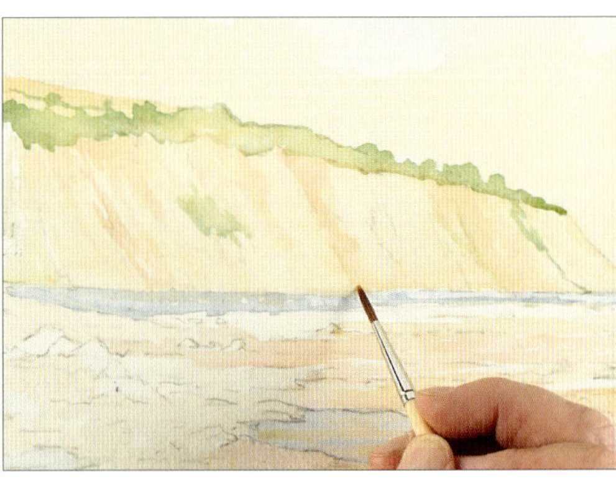

16 Reinforce the striations on the cliff with the same mix of Indian red with raw sienna.

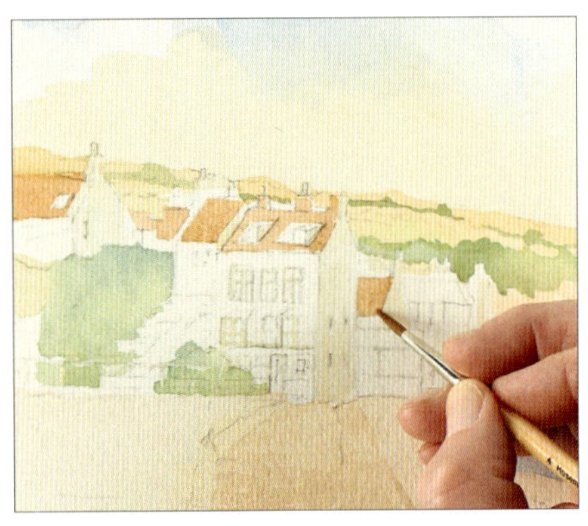

17 Begin to paint the roofs of the buildings with an orange mix of cadmium red with a little cadmium yellow added.

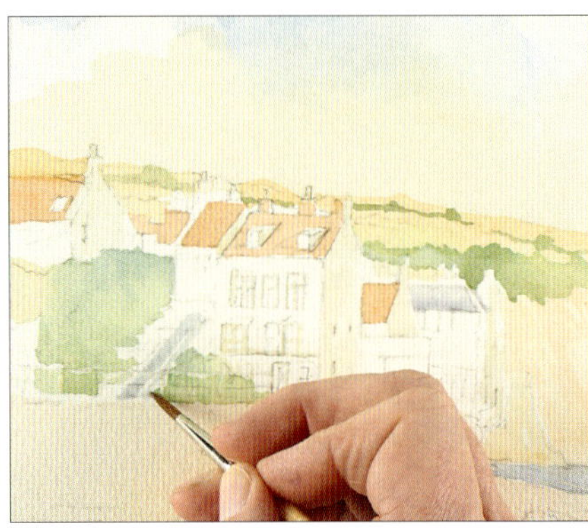

18 Lay in a light wash of Payne's grey and Winsor violet on the final roof on the right, then use pure Payne's grey to paint the walkway on the left.

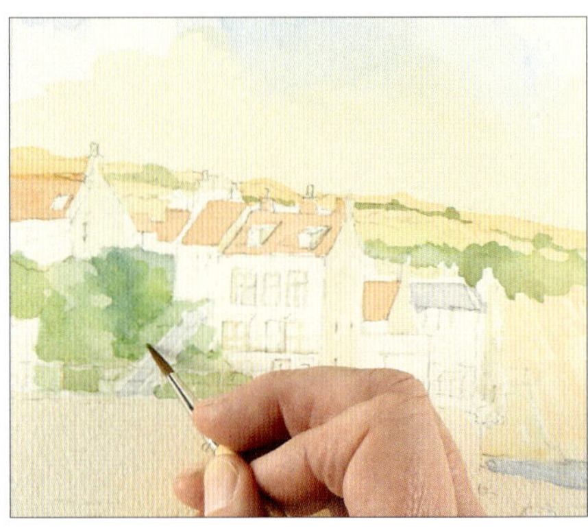

19 Reinforce the foliage between the two houses with a wash of the dark green mix (burnt umber and viridian), adding Winsor green to vary the hue.

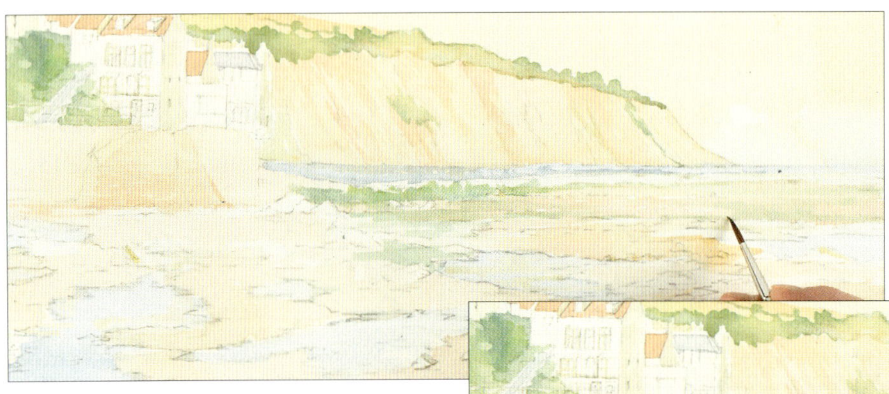

20 Lay in a dilute form of the dark green mix on the seaweed patches in the midground, adding Winsor yellow to vary the hue.

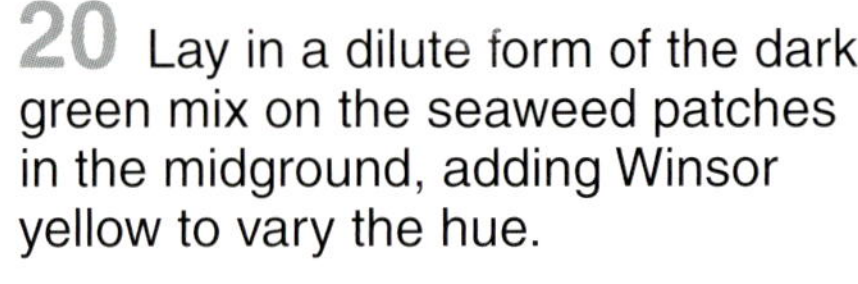

21 Paint the seaweed patches in the foreground with a less dilute dark green mix, again varying the colour with Winsor yellow.

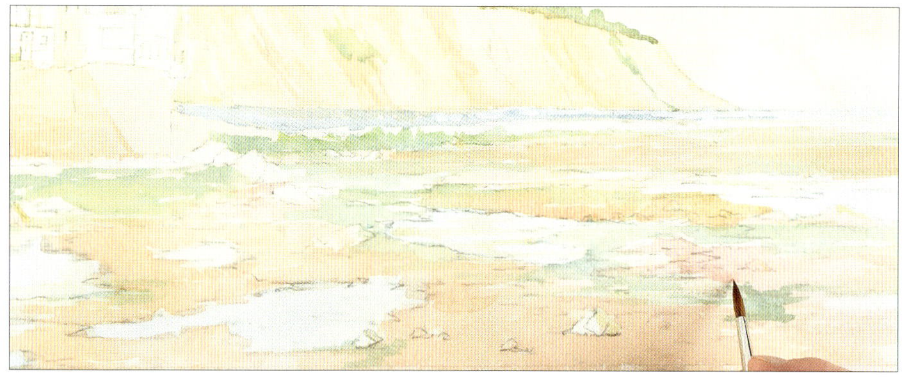

22 Using the size 6 round, reinforce the sandy area in the foreground and middle distance with the Indian red and raw sienna mix. Allow the painting to dry before continuing.

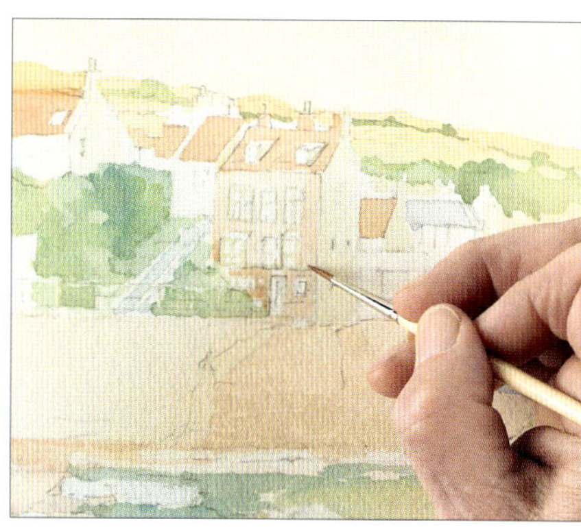

23 Swap to the size 2 round and make a stronger brown mix from Indian red and raw sienna. Use the mix to strengthen the colour at the base of the main house.

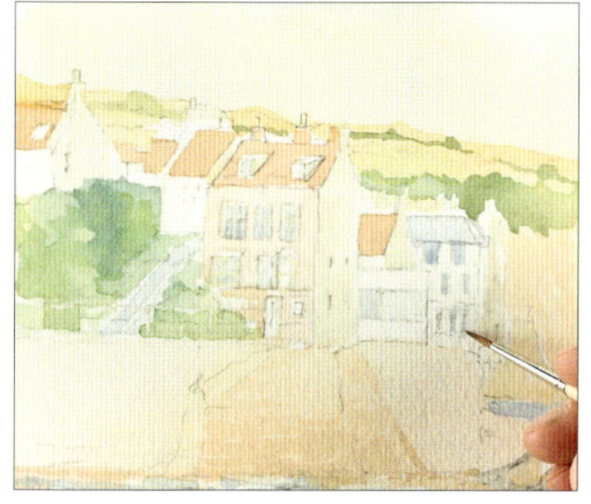

24 Use Payne's grey to paint in the windows on the houses.

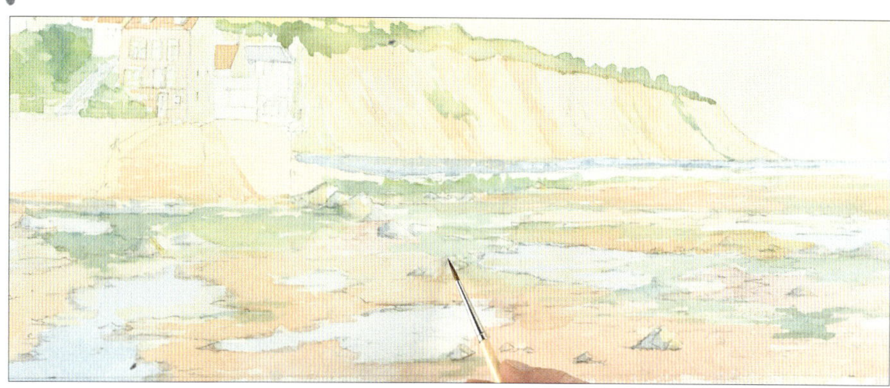

25 Begin to add some detail to the foreground and middle distance using Payne's grey, picking up the shadows of the rocks.

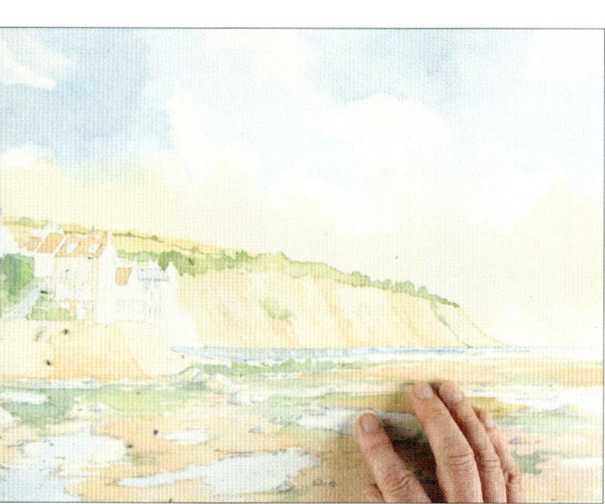

26 Allow the painting to dry completely, then use a clean finger to remove all of the masking fluid.

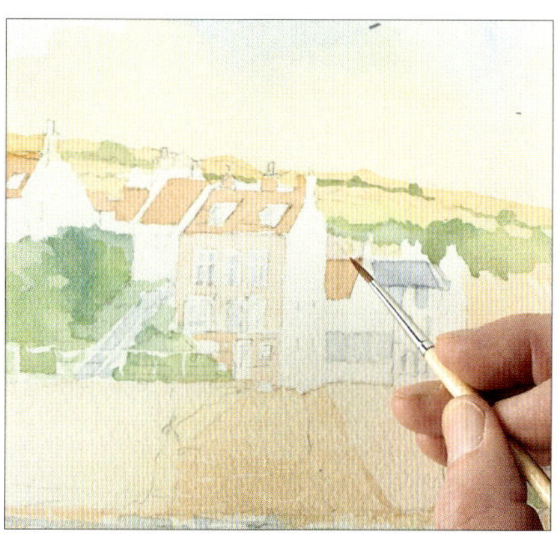

27 Return to the houses and reinforce the grey roof with a Payne's grey mix, and add in the background roof with a mix of Indian red and Payne's grey using the size 2 round.

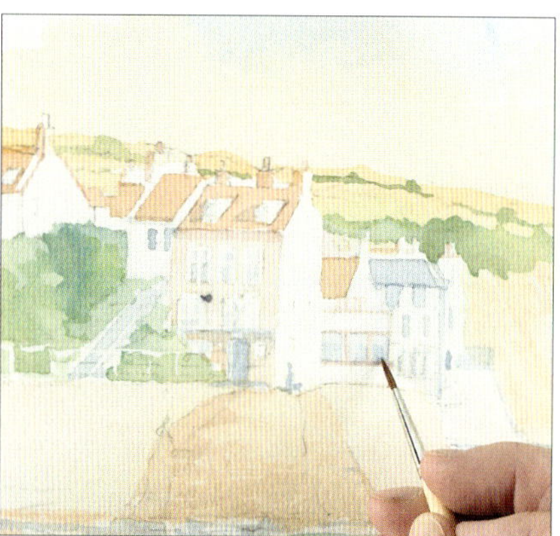

28 Develop the shadows and recesses on the buildings using dilute versions of the Indian red and Payne's grey mix and the cobalt blue and Payne's grey mix.

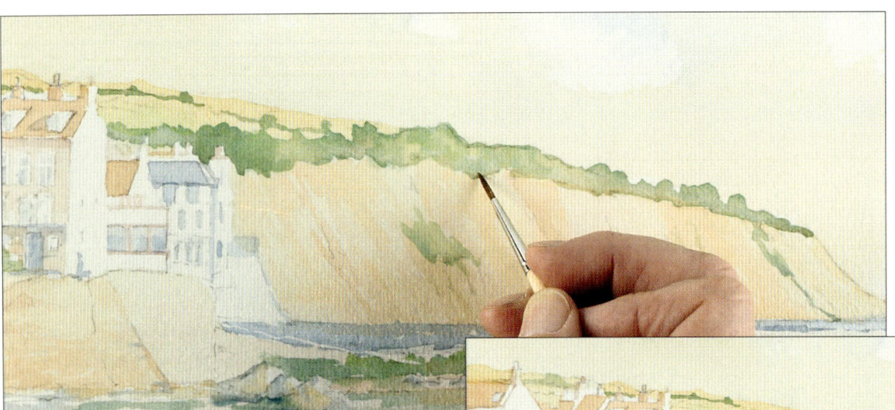

29 Develop the shadows on the background trees using the dark green mix (burnt umber and viridian).

30 Add shading and texture to the rocks in the midground and foreground with a wash of pure Payne's grey, then add a little cobalt blue to the mix and use horizontal strokes to develop the rock pools themselves.

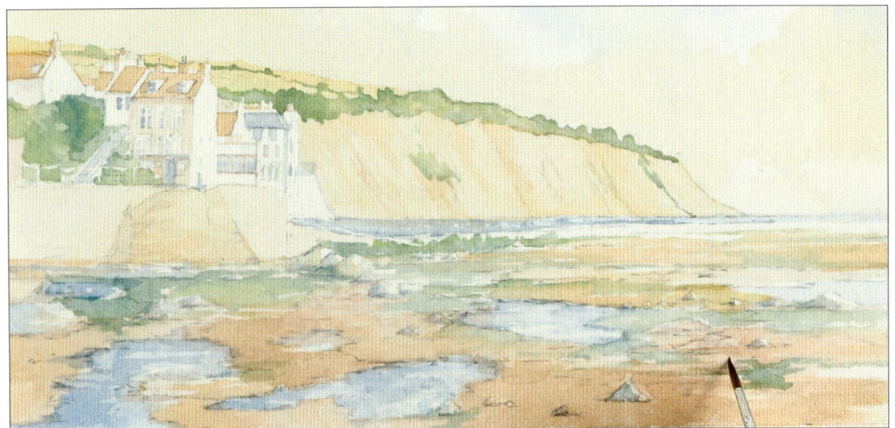

31 Switch to the size 6 round brush and make a warm mix of Indian red with raw sienna. Use loose strokes to intensify the foreground.

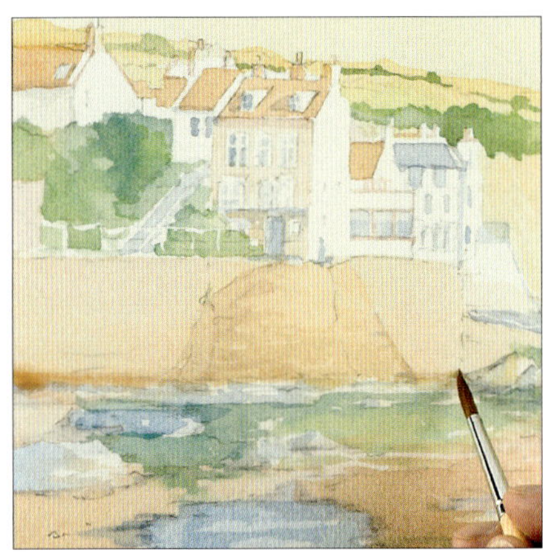

32 Wash the sea wall foundations with dilute Indian red.

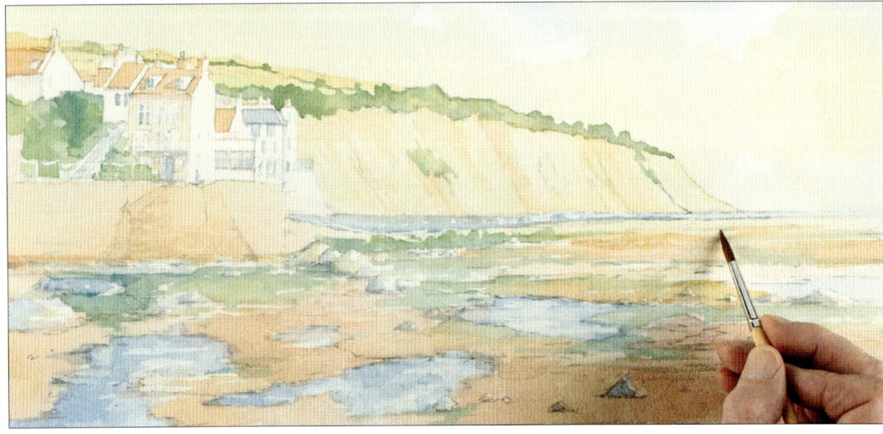

33 Strengthen the beach area in the middle ground with raw sienna.

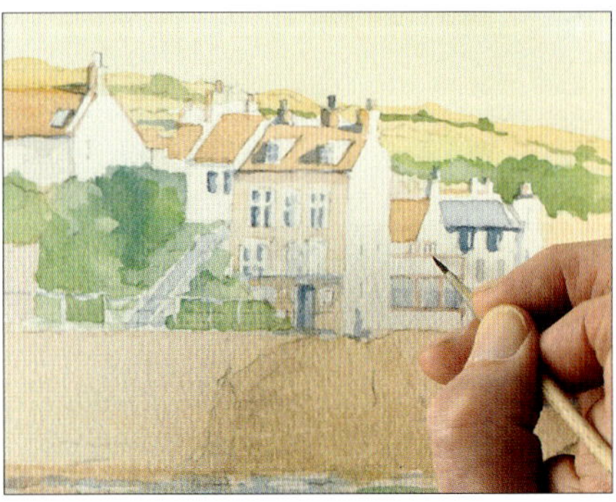

34 Use the size 1 round with Payne's grey to reinforce the shadows and make the details on the houses more crisp.

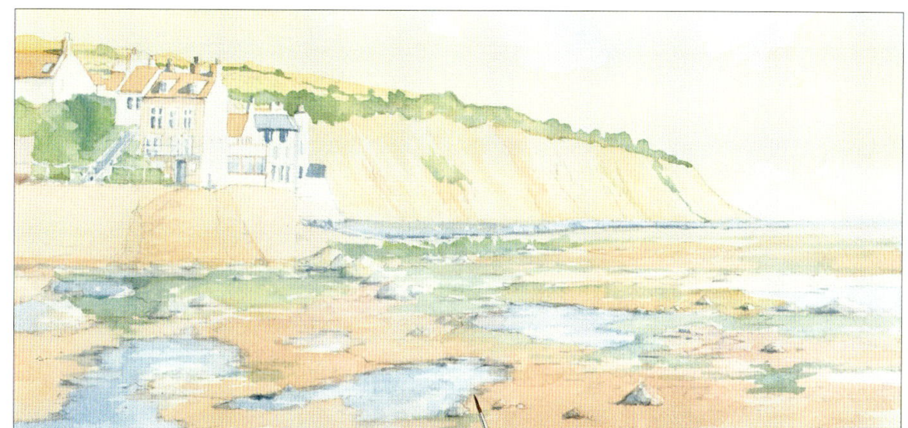

35 Continue using Payne's grey to sharpen details across the painting, reinforcing the shadows on the rocks and also darkenening the edges of the rock pools.

36 Develop the striations on the cliffs with strokes of a dilute Indian red and Payne's grey mix.

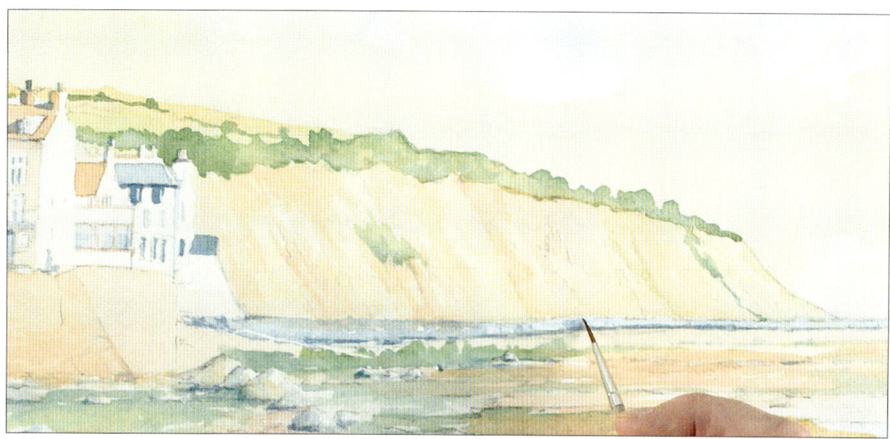

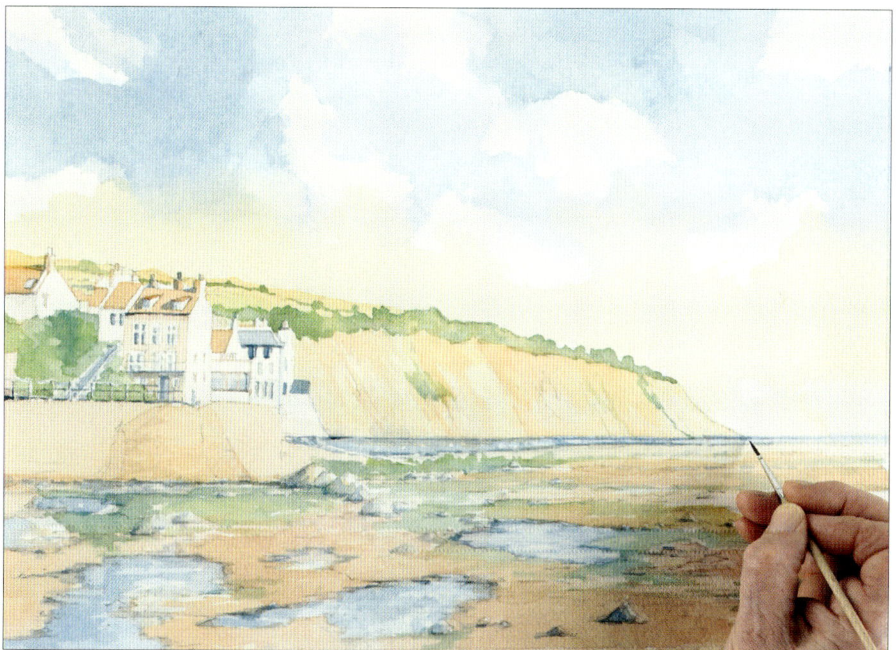

37 Add a ragged glaze of raw sienna to the top half of the cliffs, then work carefully over the painting, intensifying some of the foreground and midground shadows with glazes of Payne's grey.

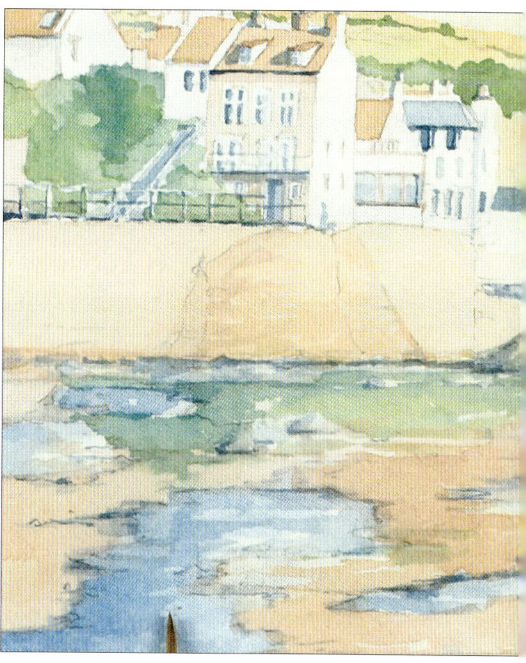

38 Draw the side of the size 4 brush, loaded with a Payne's grey and cobalt blue mix, over the rock pool on the lower left to finish.

Overleaf

The finished painting.

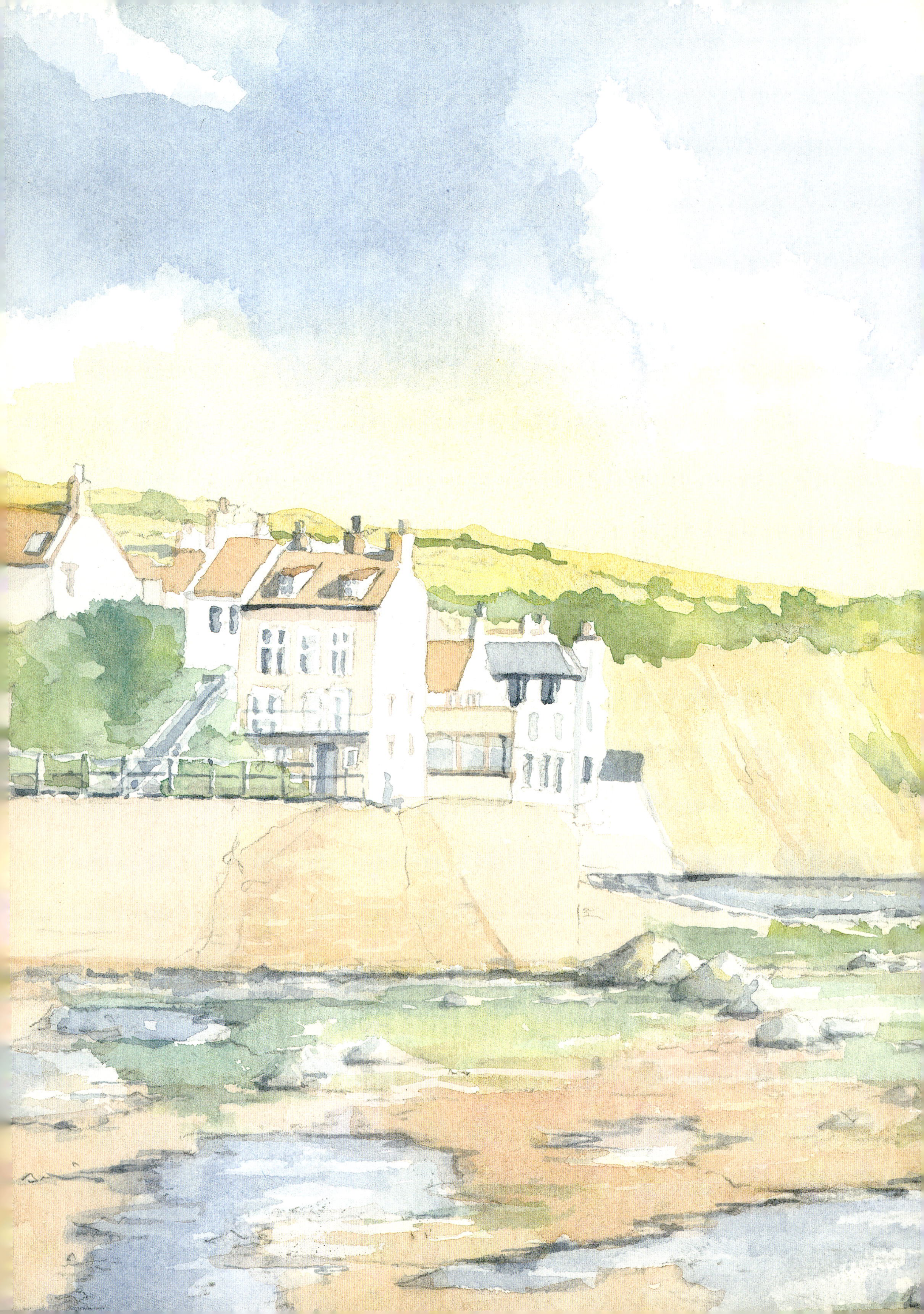

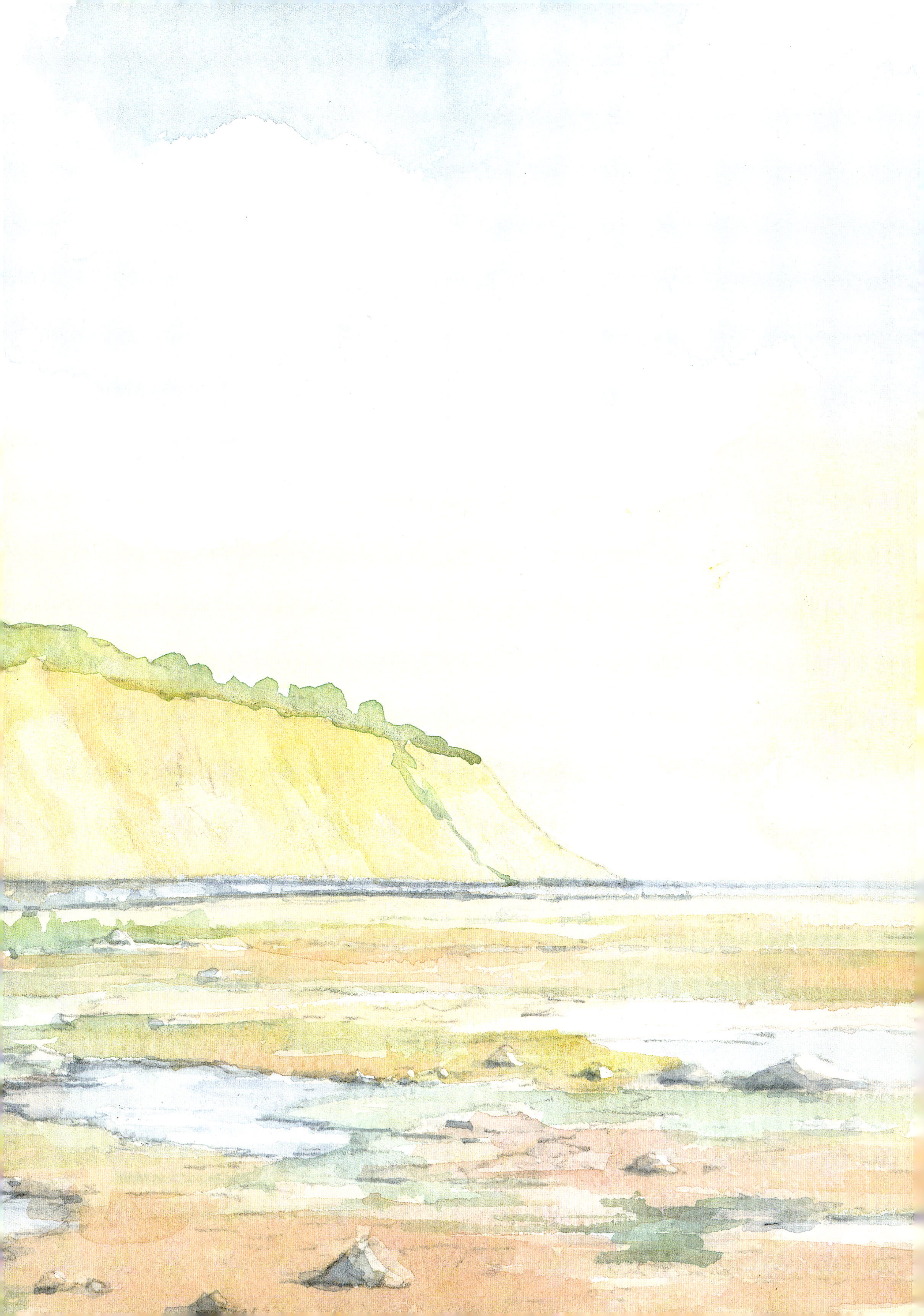

Stormy Coast

TRACING 5

This is a dramatic painting of a storm over a small coastal town. The viewpoint looks towards the derelict abbey and includes the town below. The high waves emphasise the atmosphere within the painting.

You will need

Saunders Waterford Not 640gsm (300lb) watercolour paper, 56 x 38cm (22 x 15in)

Colours: cobalt blue, raw sienna, ivory black, Payne's grey, Indian red, viridian, Winsor yellow and Winsor violet

Brushes: size 14 round, size 4 round, size 10 round, size 6 round, size 2 round and size 1 round

Masking tape and board

Masking fluid and old brush

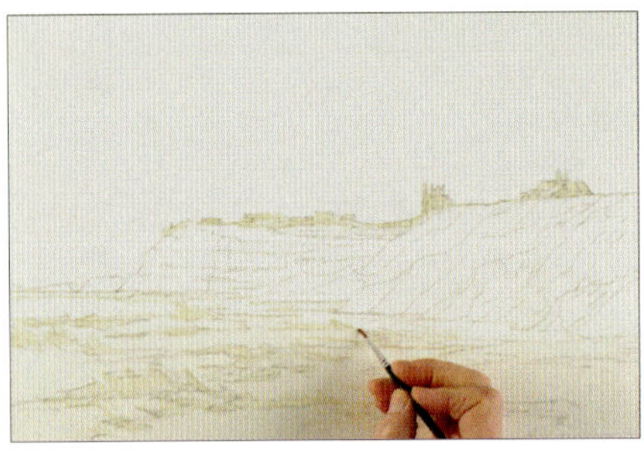

1 Run masking tape down the edges of the board to secure it in place after transferring the tracing to your paper following the instructions on page 9. Use an old brush to apply masking fluid to the ridgeline, including the buildings, and also to the crests of the waves.

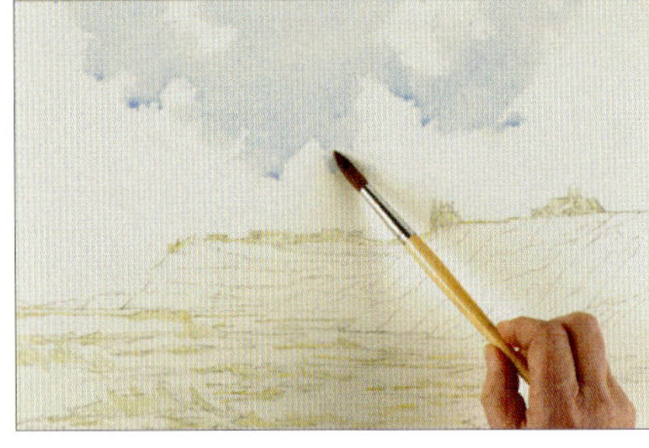

2 Establish the sky with a wash of cobalt blue, using the size 14 and brushstrokes roughly diagonal to the horizon. Leave some gaps to represent clouds, and work only the top half of the sky.

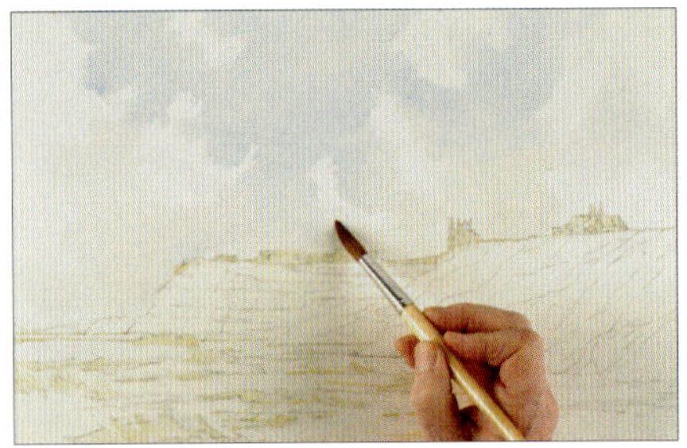

3 Draw the wet paint down to the horizon using clean water and allow to dry thoroughly before continuing.

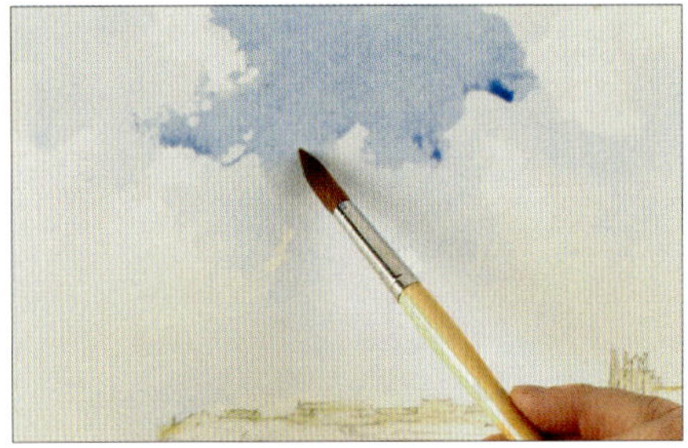

4 Prepare the following paints: raw sienna; ivory black, and a sky mix of cobalt blue and Payne's grey. Using the size 14 round with the sky mix, begin to develop a storm cloud in the centre above the town.

5 Add a tiny touch of ivory black to the mix and work the storm cloud down to the horizon.

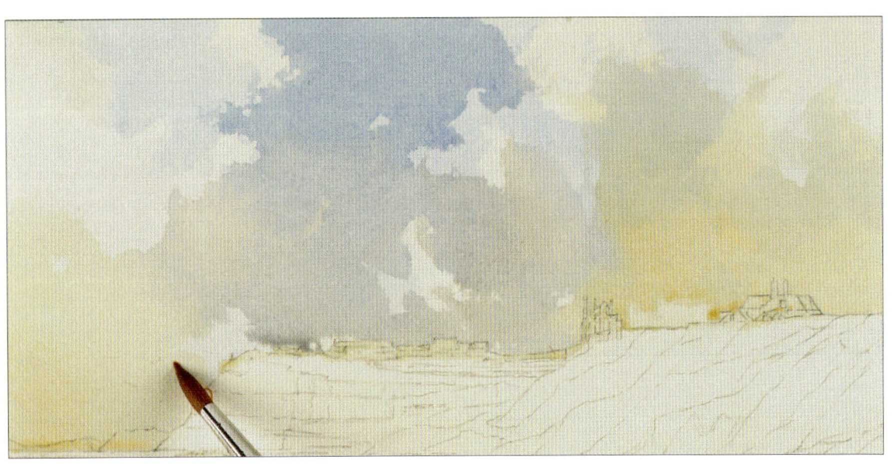

6 Work raw sienna into the left and right parts of the sky wet-in-wet. Allow the paint to dry completely before continuing.

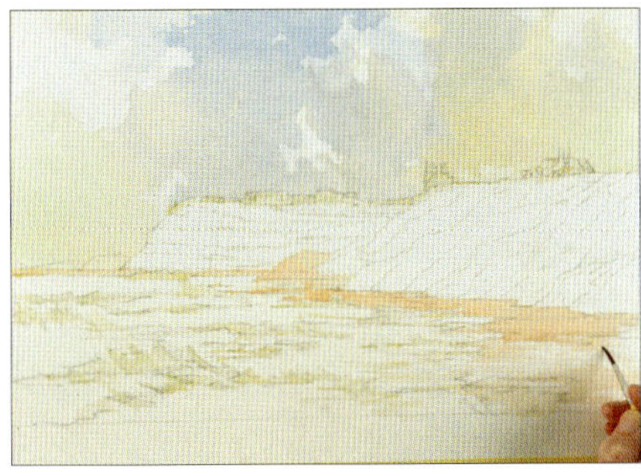

7 Switch to the size 4 round and use a mix of raw sienna and Indian red to establish the sandy area at the base of the cliffs. Create a broken effect in the foreground by drawing the brush in loose, light strokes across the lower right.

8 Using the size 10 brush, add a drop of ivory black to the cobalt blue and Payne's grey mix. Using the side of the brush, develop some more threatening storm clouds over the house on the upper right.

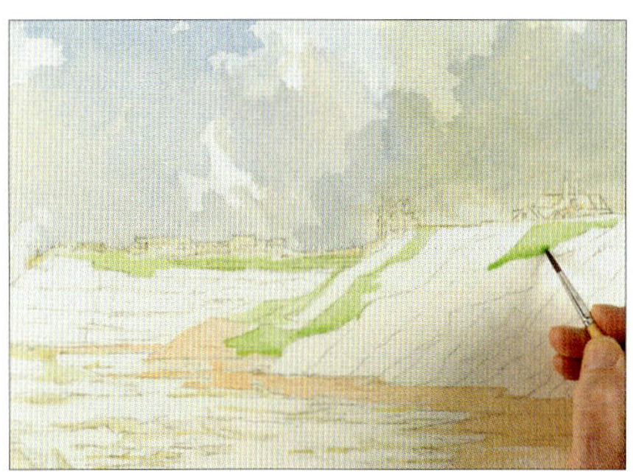

9 Prepare a green mix of viridian and Winsor yellow, and also the following colours: Indian red and raw sienna. Use the size 4 round to apply the green mix on the cliffs as shown.

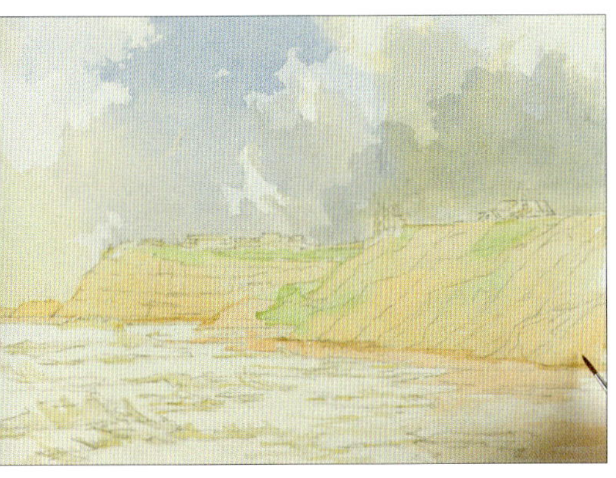

10 Drop in raw sienna over the cliffs wet-in-wet, dropping in touches of Indian red and the green mix to vary the tone.

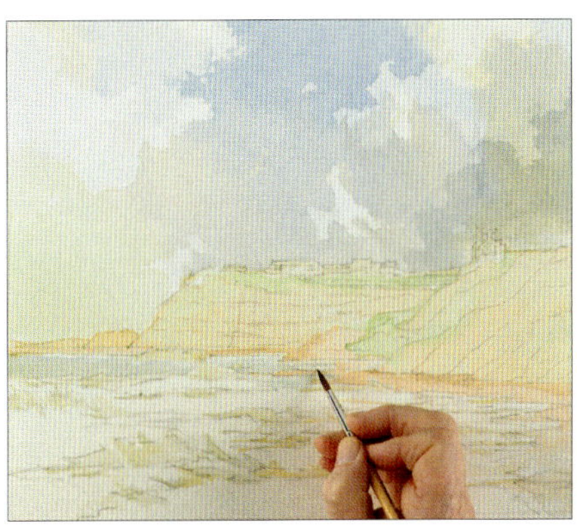

11 Prepare viridian, cobalt blue, Payne's grey and raw sienna. Swap to the size 6 brush and lay in cobalt blue with a little raw sienna and Payne's grey on the sea by the horizon.

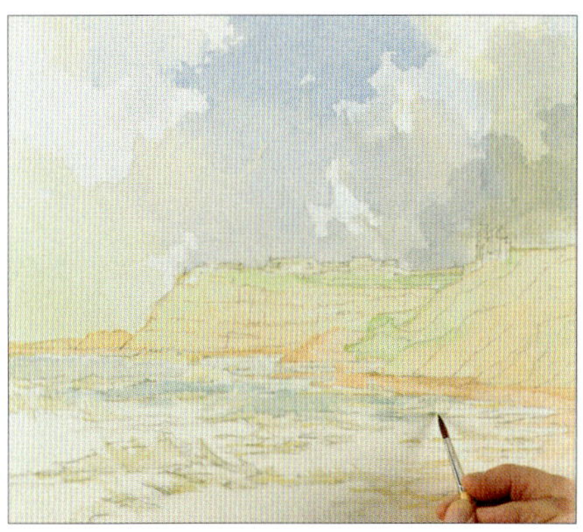

12 Add some viridian and raw sienna to the mix as you advance to the midground.

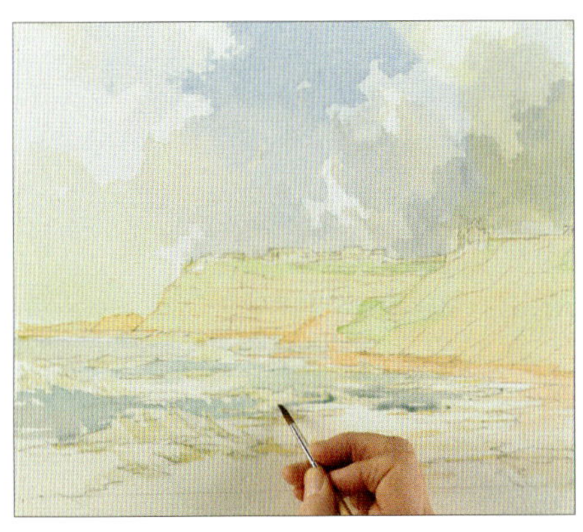

13 Use a mix of cobalt blue and Payne's grey with a touch of viridian as you advance still further.

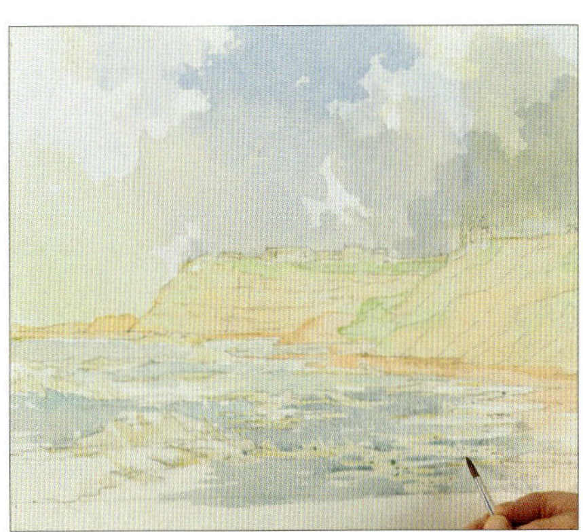

14 Use a mix of cobalt blue and Payne's grey to build up the central and right-hand areas of the foreground with horizontal brushstrokes.

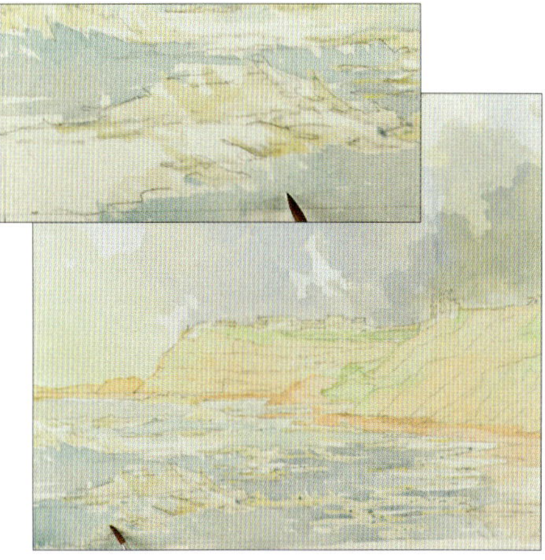

15 Add a touch of viridian to the cobalt blue and Payne's grey mix and paint the underside of the wave on the left of the foreground (see inset), before using the same mix to finish the foreground.

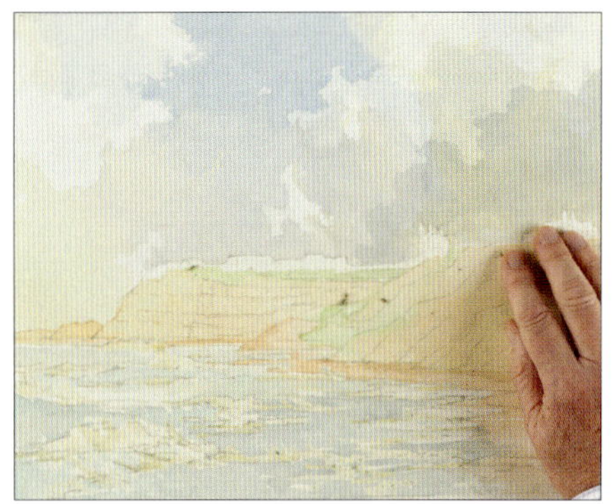

16 Leaving the masking fluid on the sea untouched, carefully remove the masking fluid from the top of the cliffs and buildings.

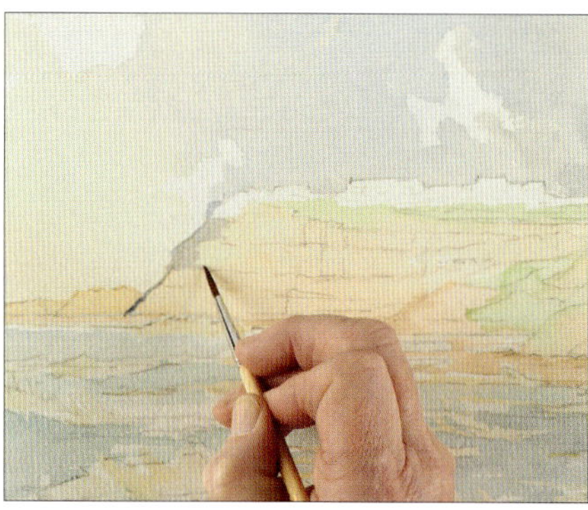

17 Use a size 4 brush to apply a grey mix of Winsor violet, Payne's grey and cobalt blue to the edge of the cliff on the left, then draw the colour out towards the right.

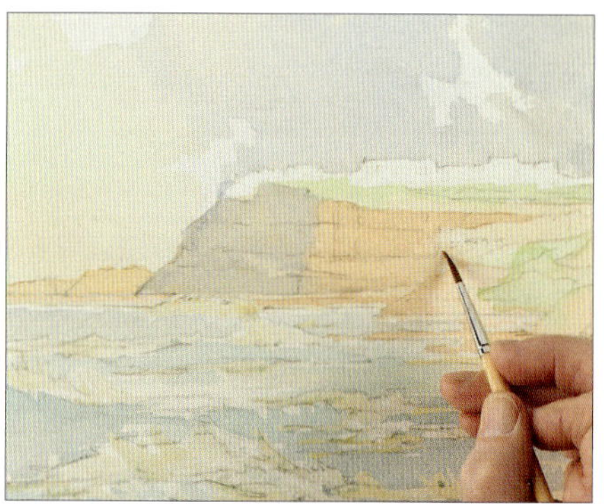

18 Draw the mix over the left-hand part of the background cliff, then paint the central part with a warm mix of raw sienna and Indian red.

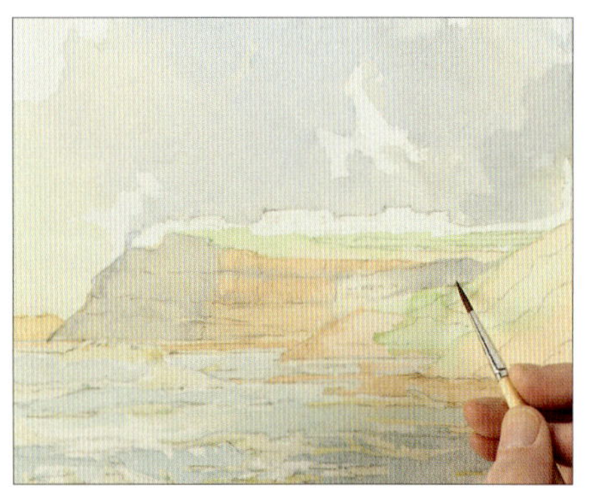

19 Use the grey mix to add striations wet-in-wet to the middle part of the background cliff, then fill in the right-hand side with the grey mix again.

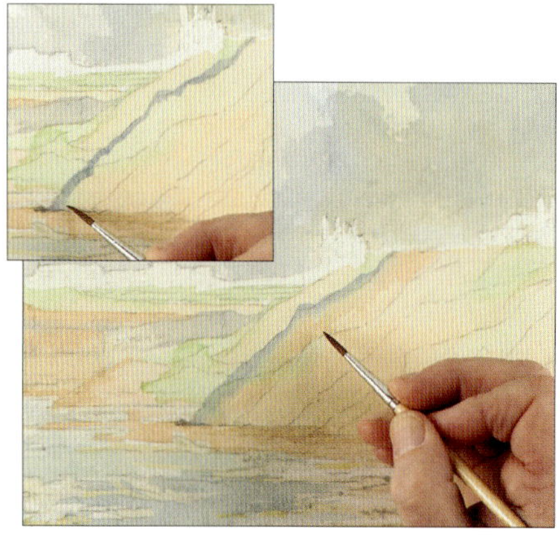

20 Edge the foreground cliff with the grey mix (see inset), then work wet-in-wet to add the warm mix to the right.

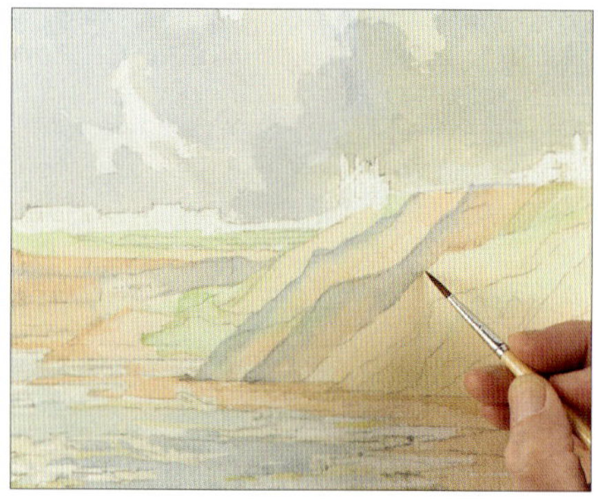

21 Allow the first section to dry, then use the lines of the tracing as a guideline to show you where to draw the next line of the grey mix. Build up the next section of the cliff in the same way as the first.

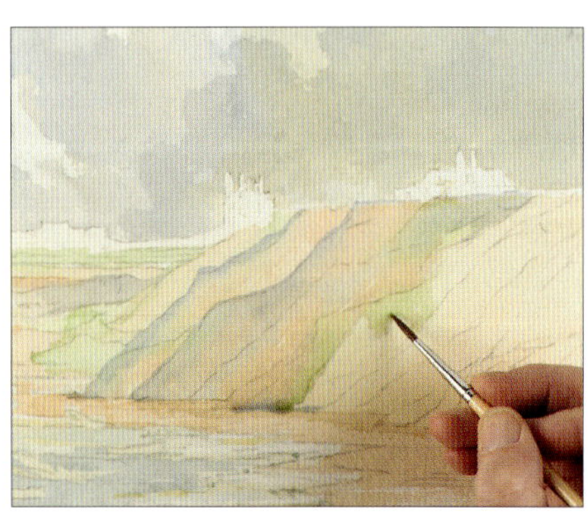

22 Being sure to allow each section to dry before continuing, work to the centre of the cliff. Add in a section using a viridian and Winsor yellow mix, to create some interest and variety.

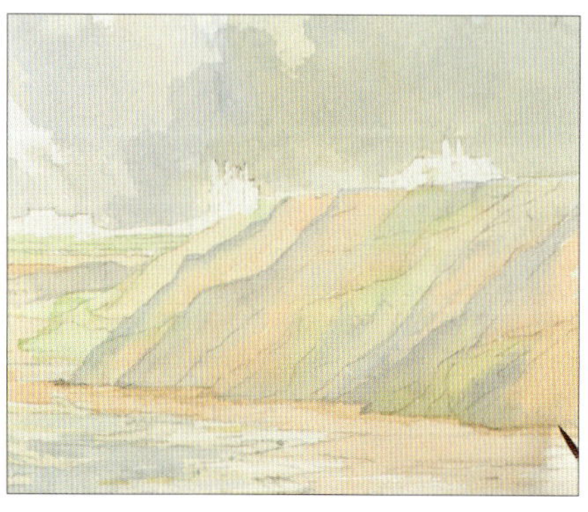

23 Work the right-hand side of the cliff in the same way, using the grey and warm mixes.

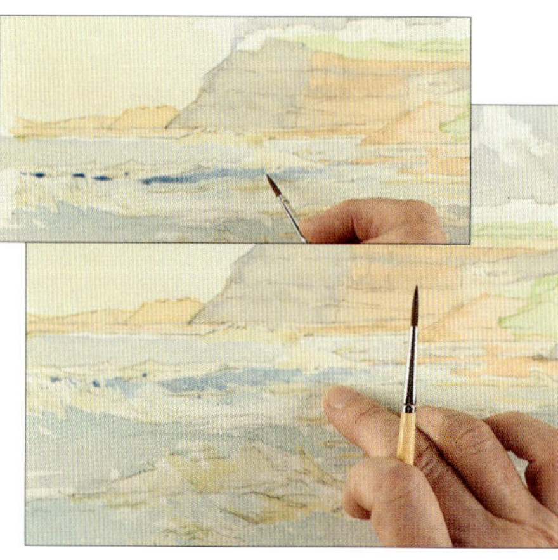

24 Using a mix of cobalt blue and Payne's grey, draw a fine line under the cresting wave (see inset), then draw it down diagonally using a clean finger.

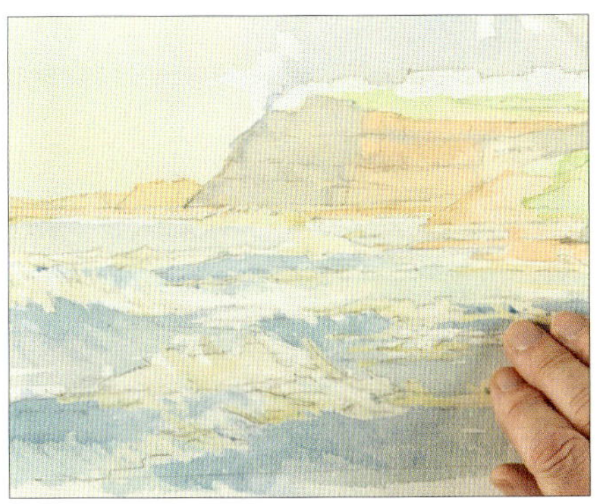

25 Shade the other cresting waves in the same way, then allow them to dry.

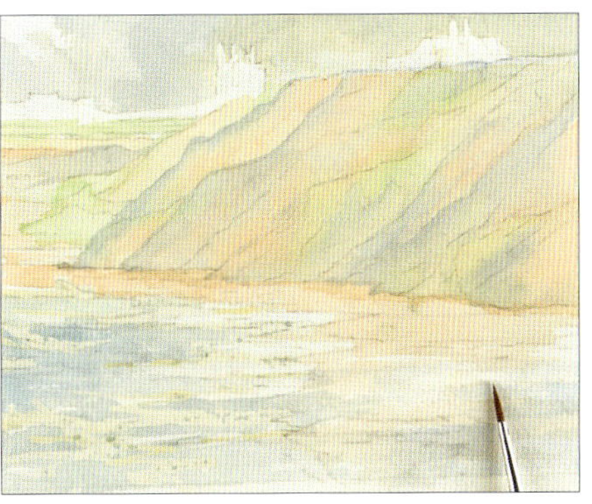

26 Use the same mix and drag the side of the brush from the right to the left to produce a texture over part of the beach.

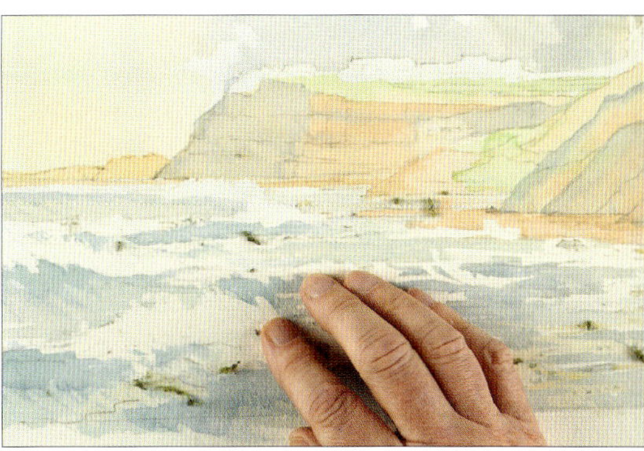

27 Carefully remove the remaining masking fluid from the waves to reveal the fresh clean paper.

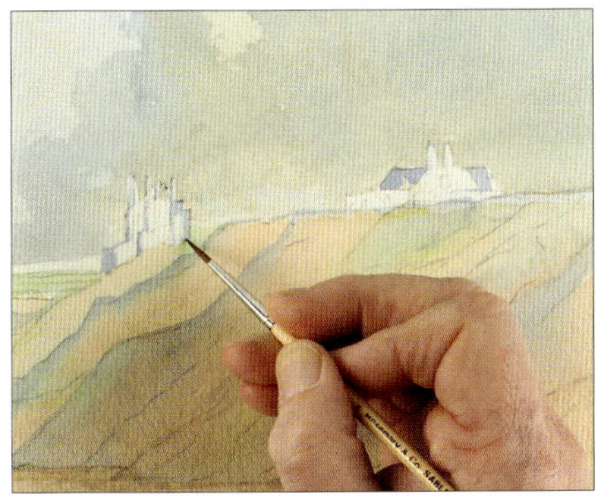

28 Using the size 2 brush, begin to detail the house and ruined abbey on the upper right with the grey mix of cobalt blue and Payne's grey. Keep the shadows on the left away from the light source.

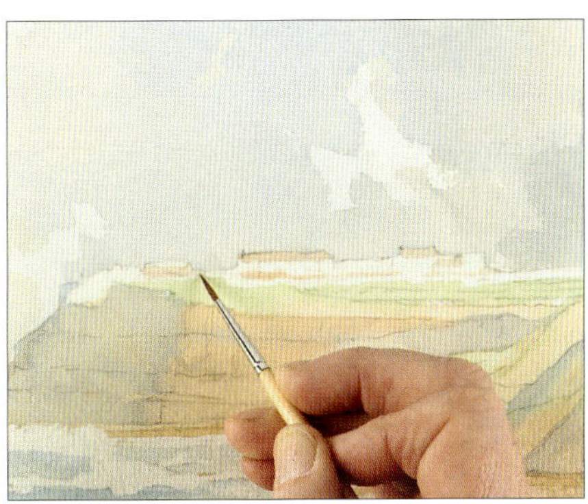

29 Use the warm mix (raw sienna and Indian red) to begin to detail the buildings on the left-hand side in the background.

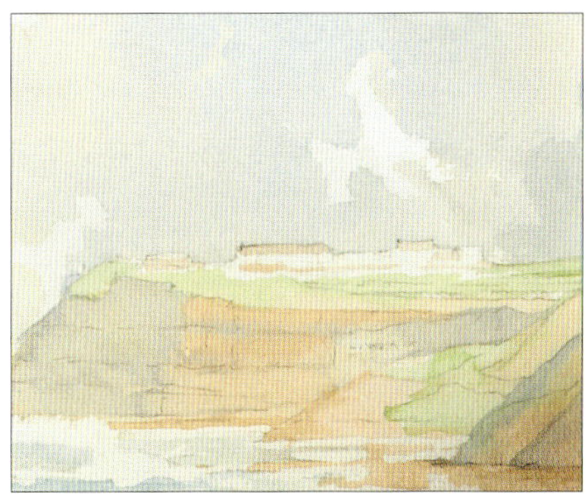

30 Fill in the foliage in the background around the distant buildings with a mix of viridian and Winsor yellow.

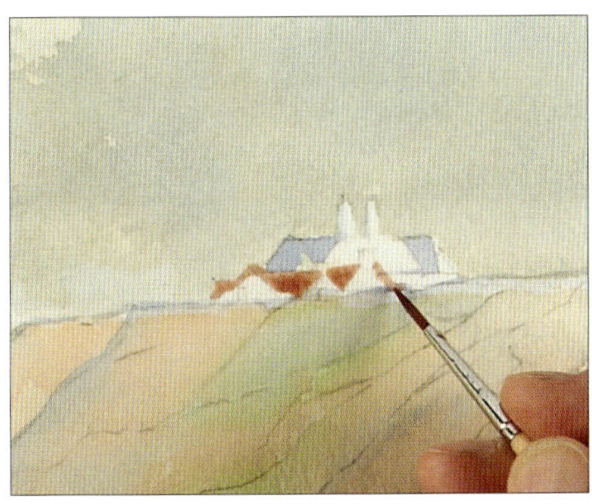

31 Add more Indian red to the warm mix to block in the roofs in front of the foreground house.

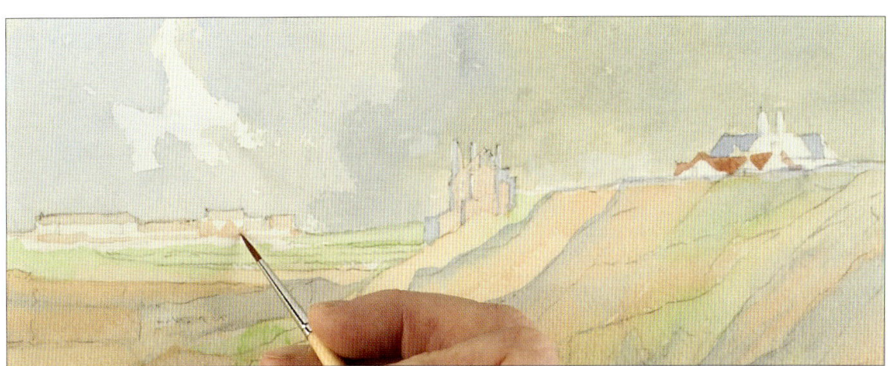

32 Block in the abbey and the background buildings with a dilute mix of raw sienna with a tiny touch of Indian red.

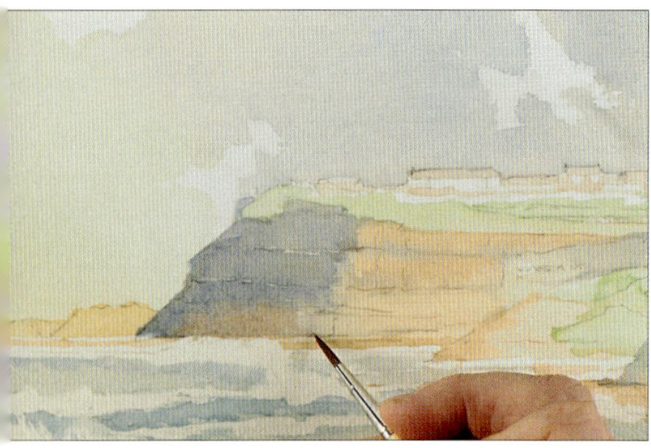

33 Change to the size 4 round and begin to texture the background cliffs with various touches of Winsor violet, cobalt blue and Payne's grey worked wet-in-wet. Leave some lighter spaces, and aim for a rocky effect. Work a little of the warm mix (Indian red and raw sienna) in at the base.

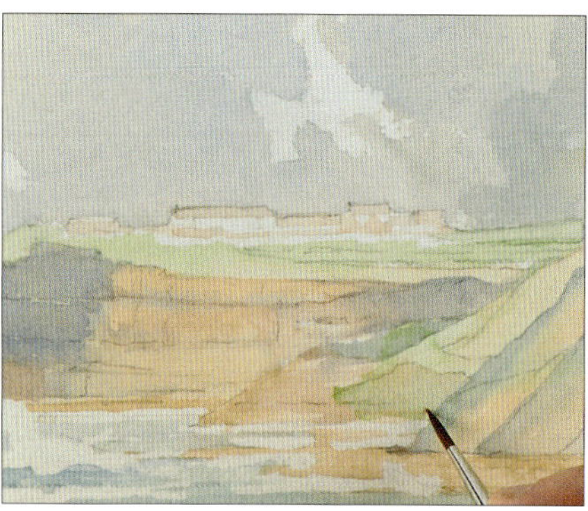

34 Using the same colours, accentuate the striations and darker areas in the central part of the background cliff.

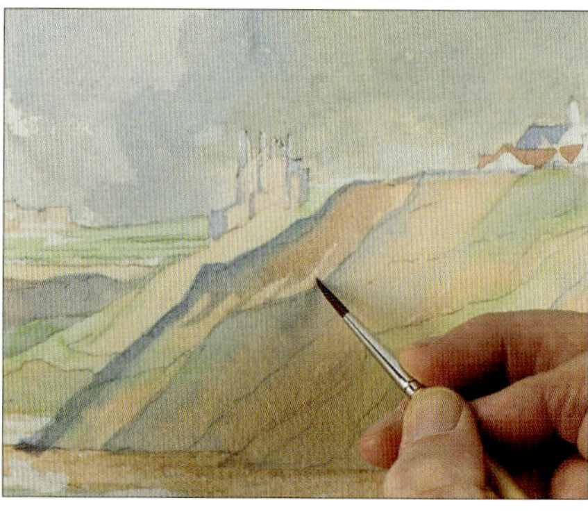

35 Using the grey mix of cobalt blue and Payne's grey to strengthen the edge of the foreground cliff, then work in strokes of the warm mix wet-in-wet. Leave patches of the previous layer showing through.

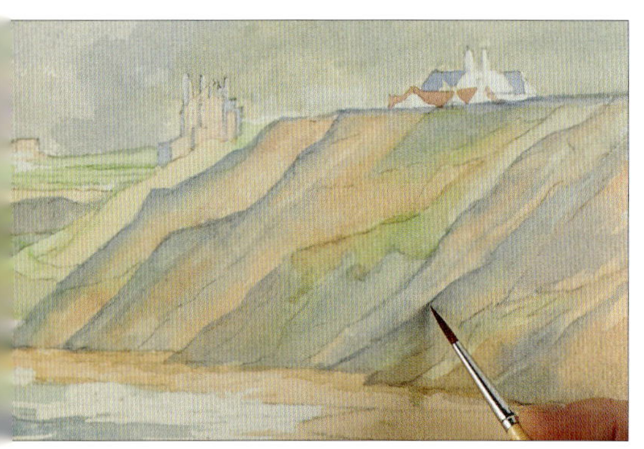

36 Strengthen and sharpen the shadows and edges of the rest of the foreground cliffs in the same way, allowing the sections to dry in turn to avoid the edges softening and bleeding into one another.

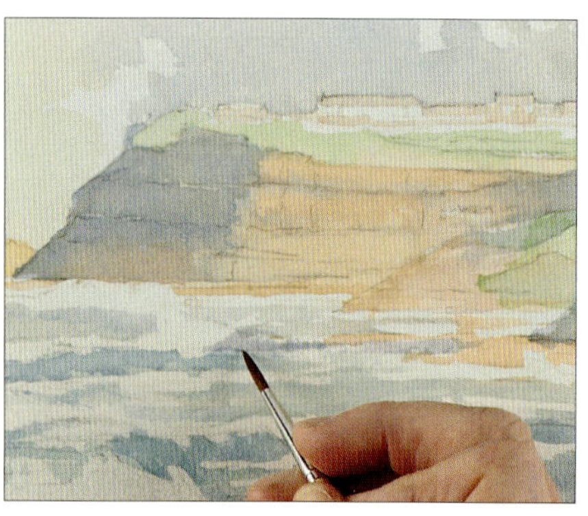

37 Paint in the peninsula using Winsor violet, cobalt blue and Payne's grey, working wet-in-wet.

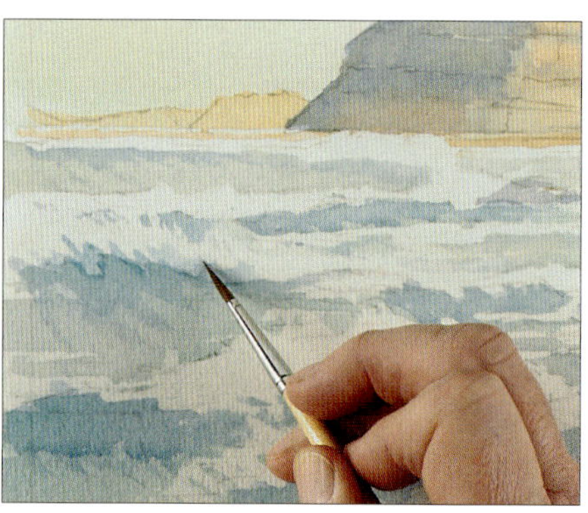

38 Mix cobalt blue with a little viridian and add short, diagonal strokes of the mix at the base of the wave crest in the midground on the right.

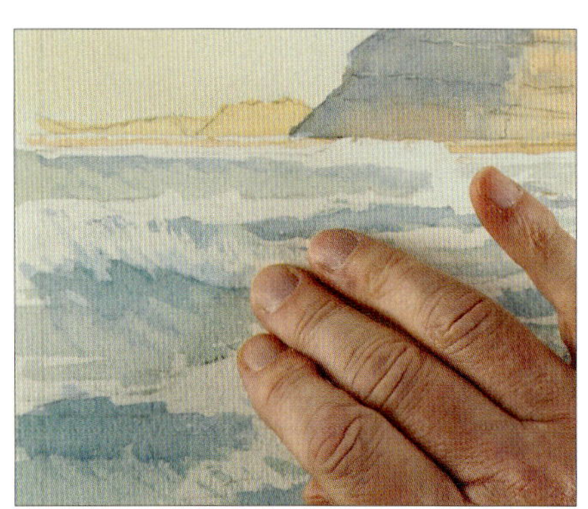

39 Use a clean finger to draw the wet paint upwards to create a fresh appearance to the base of the wave.

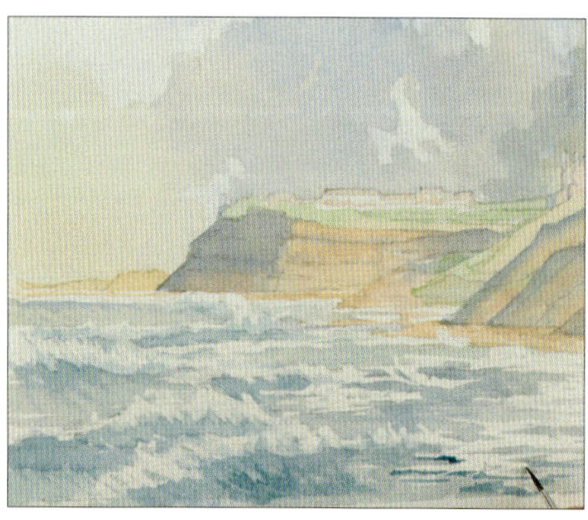

40 Continue to detail the other wave crests in the same way, making tiny changes of pigment to capture the effect of the stormy water.

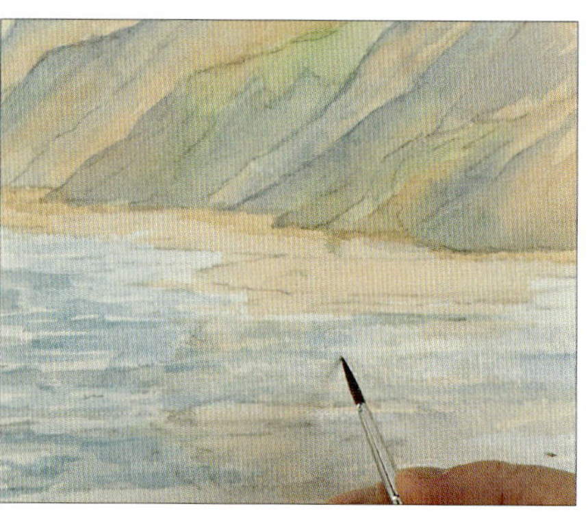

41 Use the tip of the brush to add some short, broken, horizontal strokes of the same colour over the beach on the right.

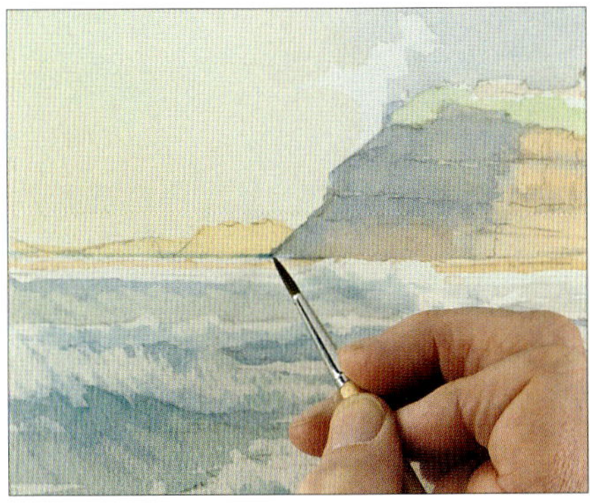

42 Reinforce the horizon with a stroke of the grey mix of Payne's grey and coablt blue.

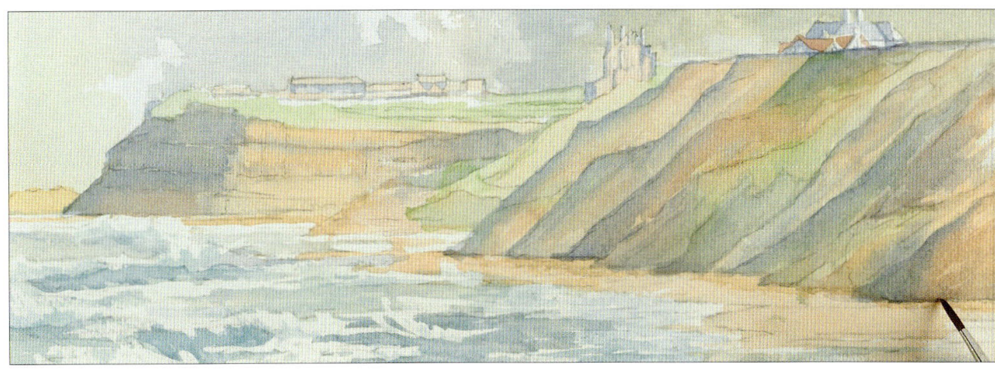

43 Use the same grey mix to add the sides and details to all of the buildings. Ensure the cliffs are absolutely dry and add further glazes across them with the same grey and warm mixes, being careful to reinforce each area.

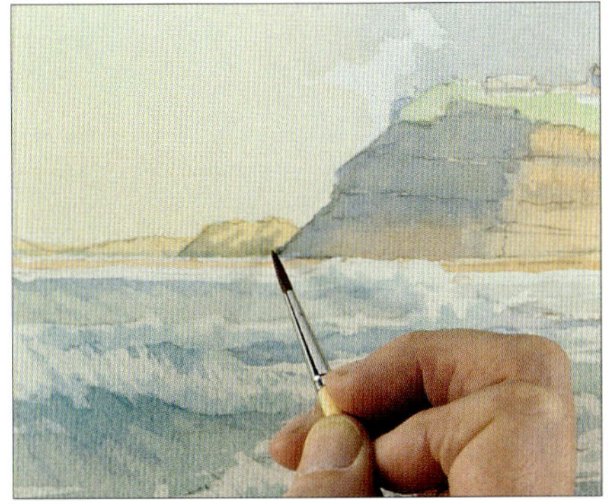

44 Use a mix of Winsor violet, cobalt blue and Payne's grey worked wet-in-wet to paint the distant headland on the horizon.

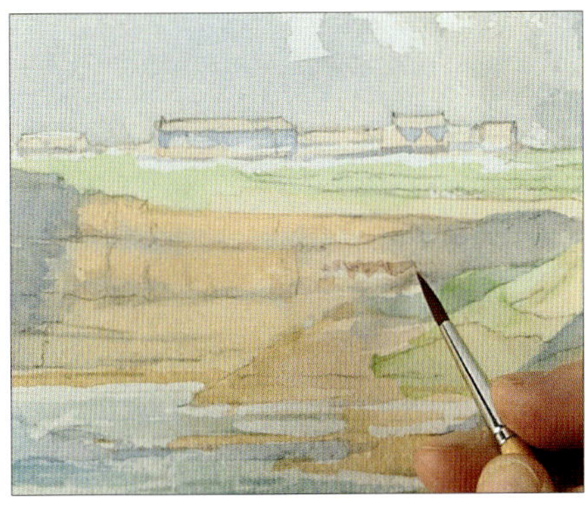

45 Paint the roofs in between the two areas of cliffs with Indian red, then draw a fine line of the grey mix along the striations on the cliff to lead the eye to the small buildings.

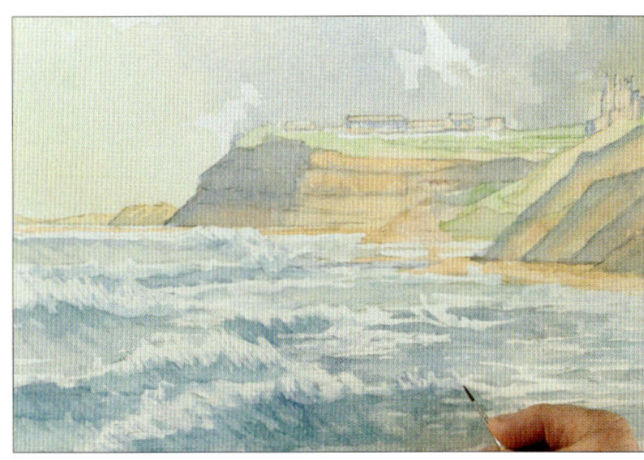

46 Further soften the harsh white areas left by the masking fluid on the sea, using the tip of the size 1 brush to add tiny strokes of the Winsor violet, cobalt blue and Payne's grey mix to enhance the undersides of the crests of the waves.

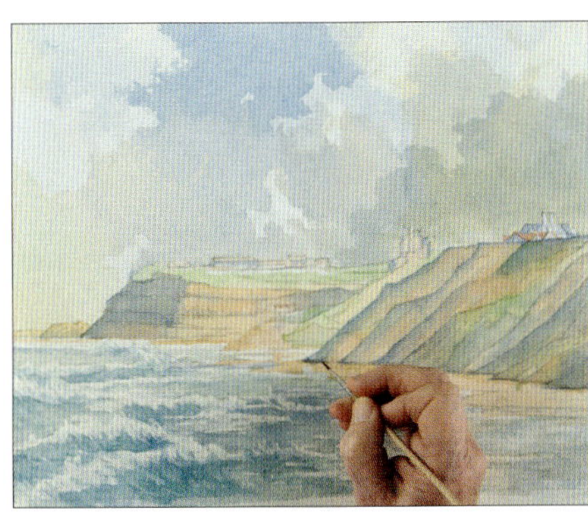

47 Use the same mix to make small adjustments across the painting, strengthening shadows and adding suggestions of texture to the rocky areas.

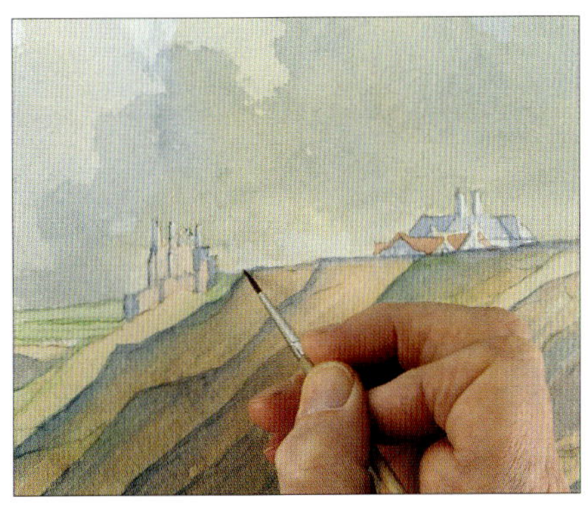

48 Reinforce the edges of the buildings with the same brush and mix, to emphasise their structure.

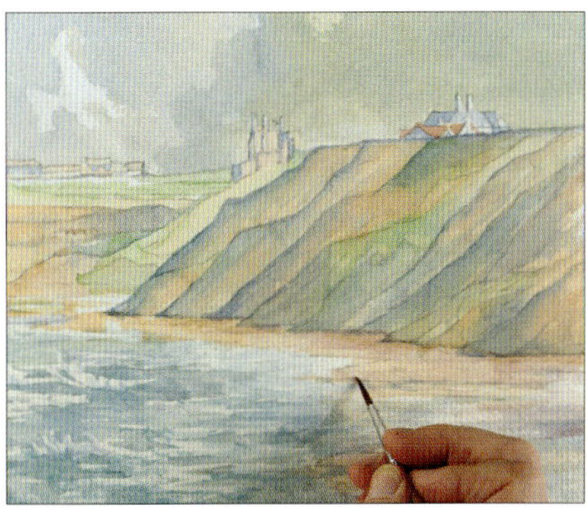

49 Use the size 4 round to add horizontal strokes of an Indian red and Winsor violet mix to the beach.

Overleaf

The finished painting.

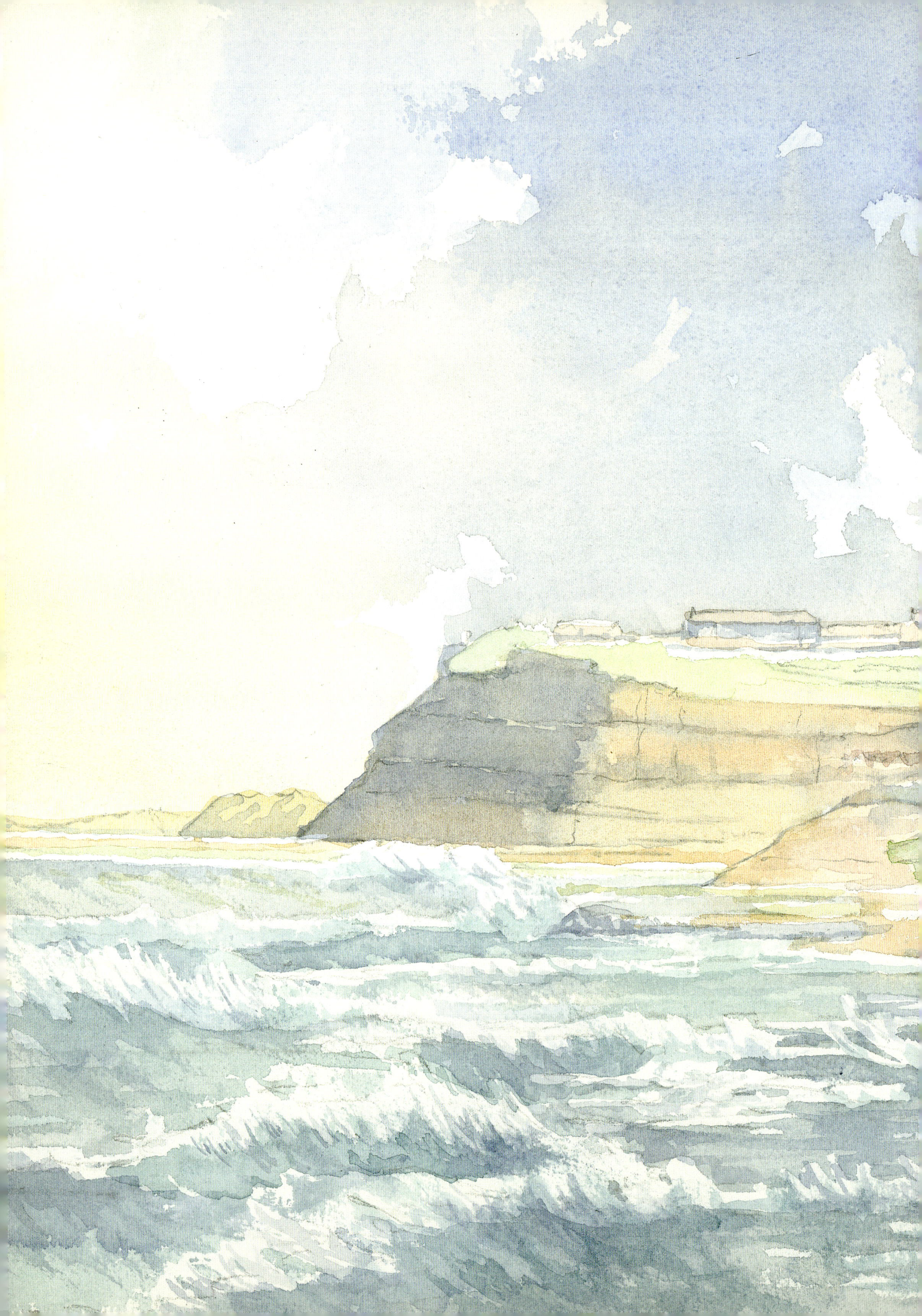

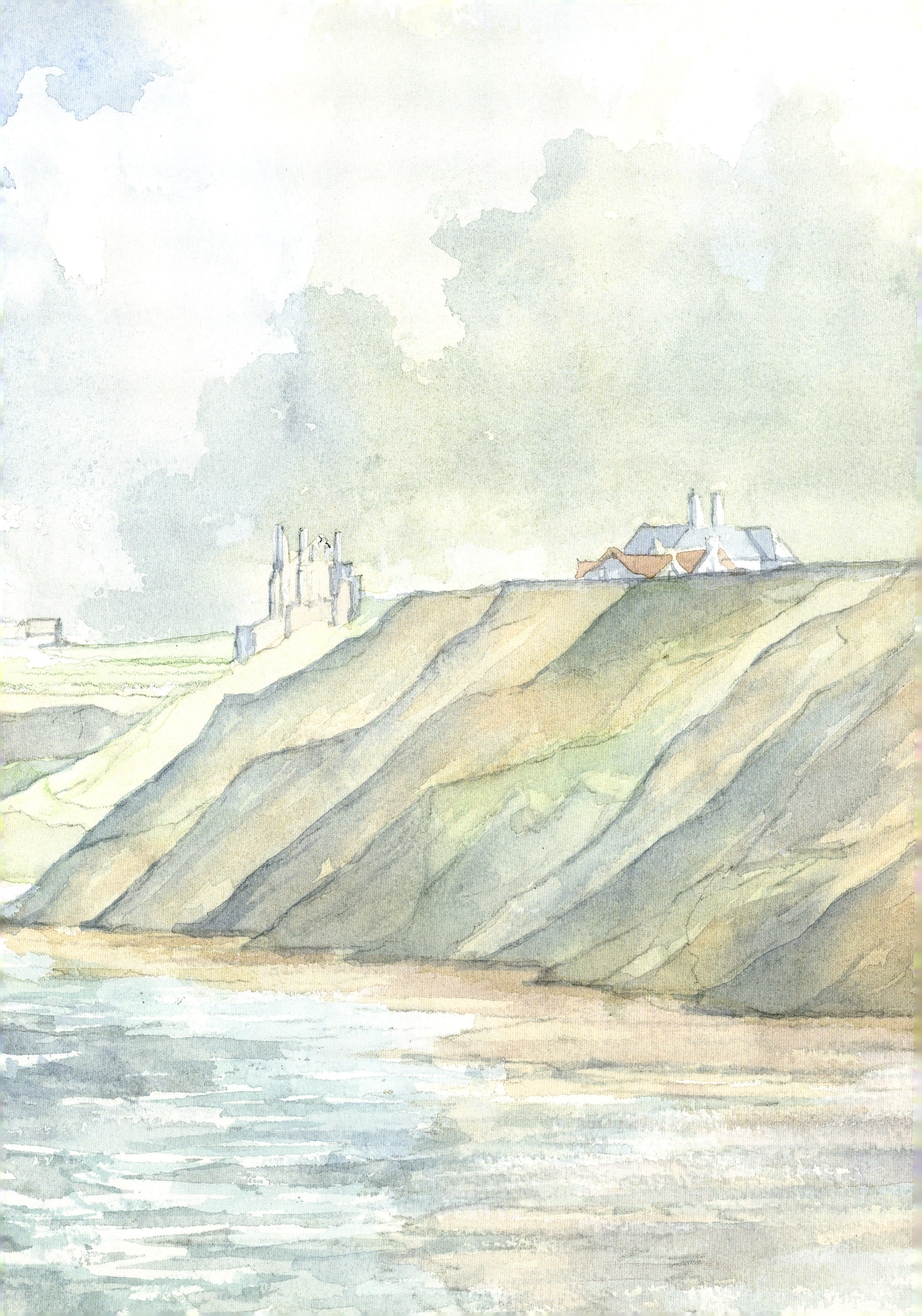

Index

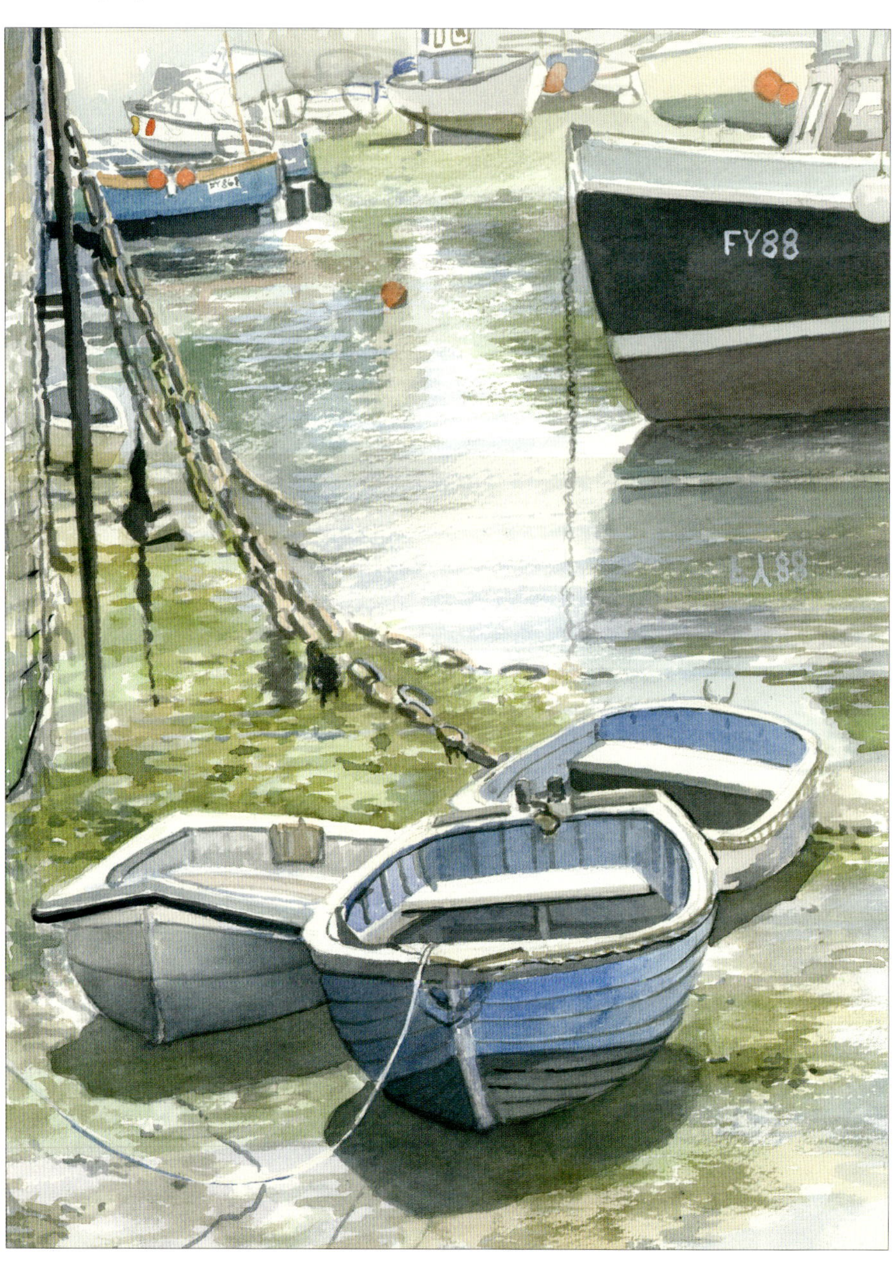

Boat in the Inner Harbour

56 x 38cm (22 x 15in)

This painting details some small vessels in the harbour of Mevagissey, Cornwall.

For a complete list of all our books see

www.searchpress.com

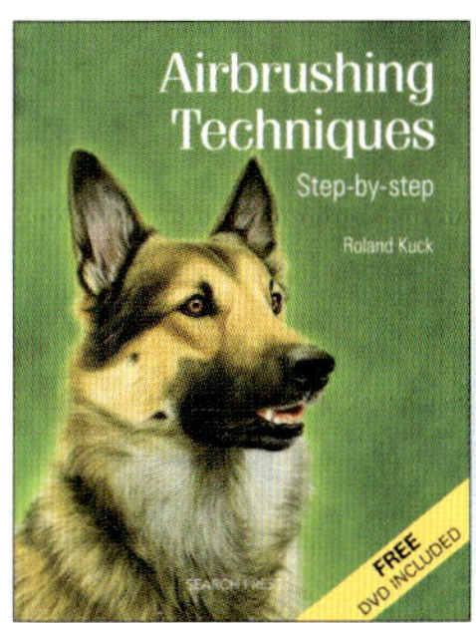

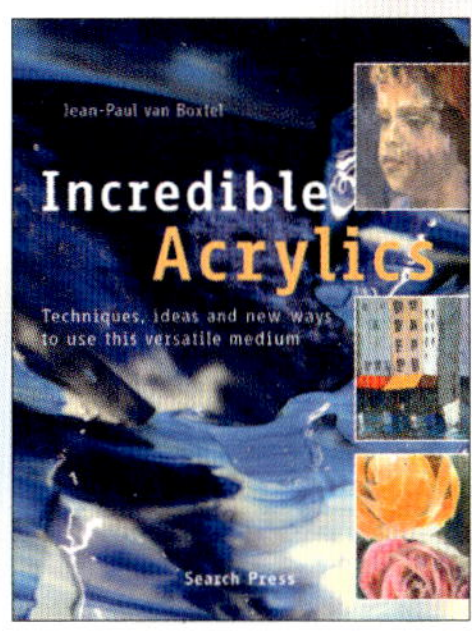

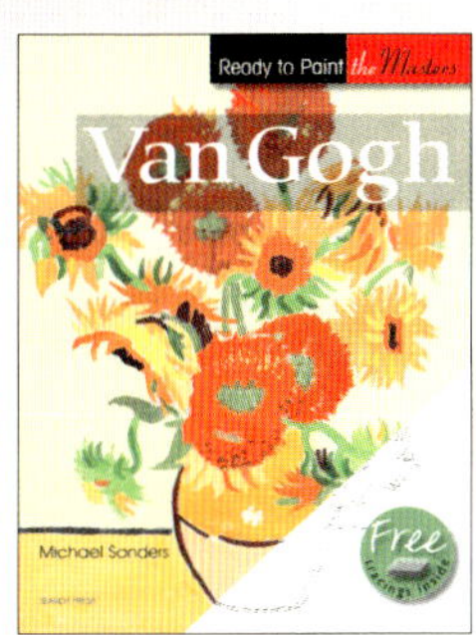

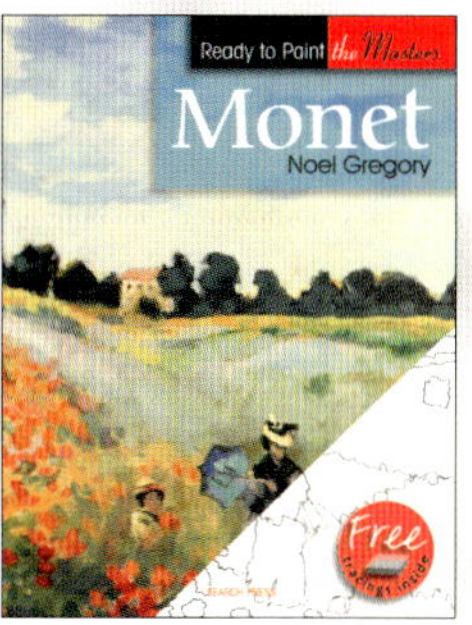

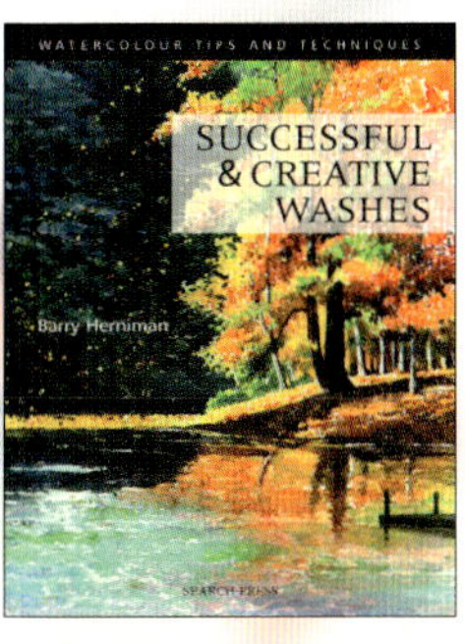

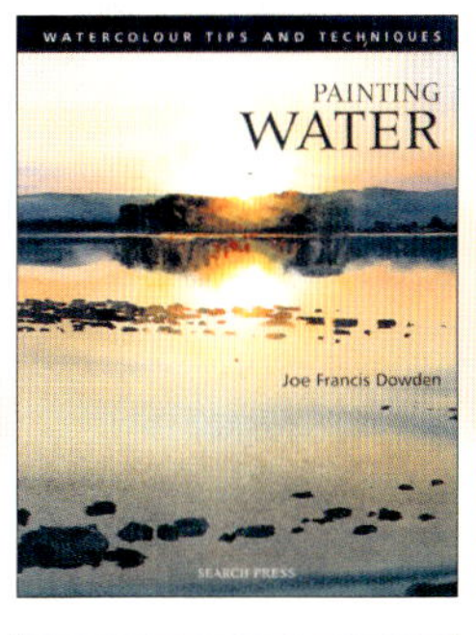

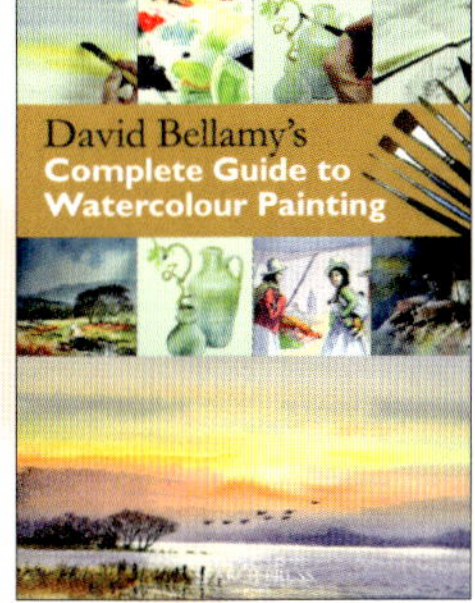

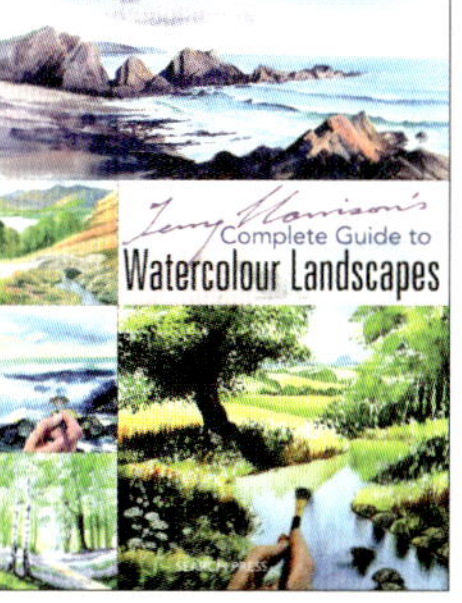

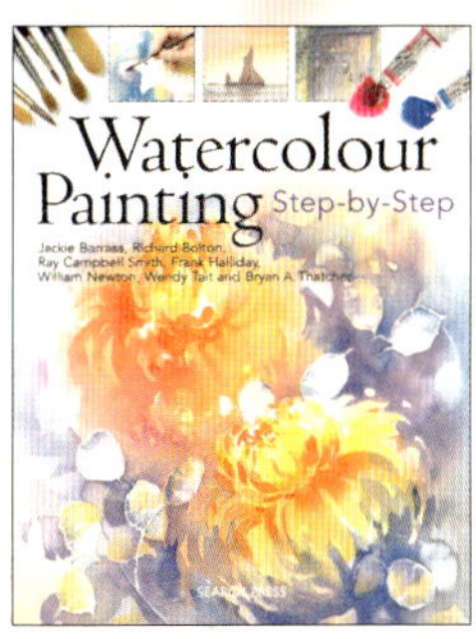

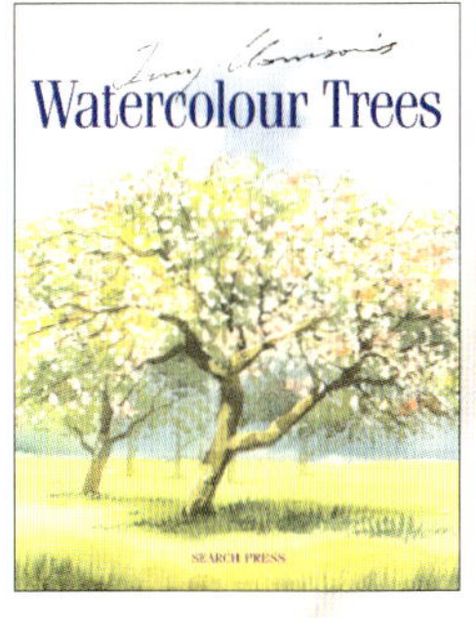

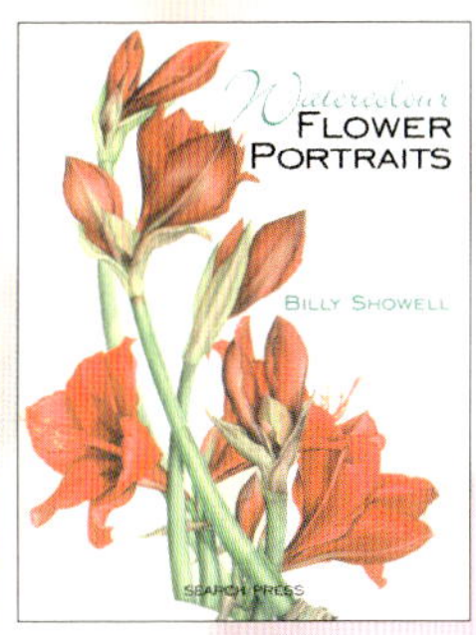

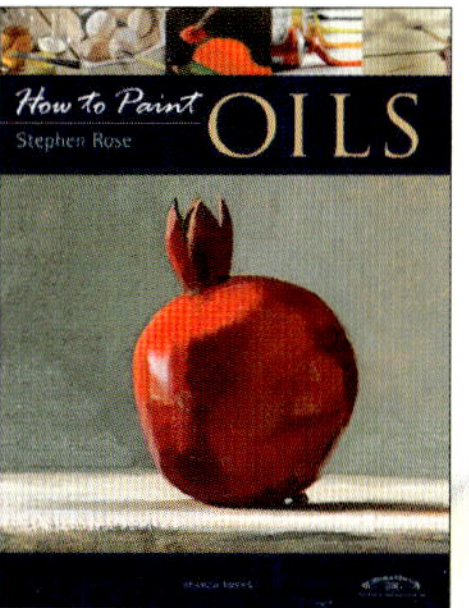

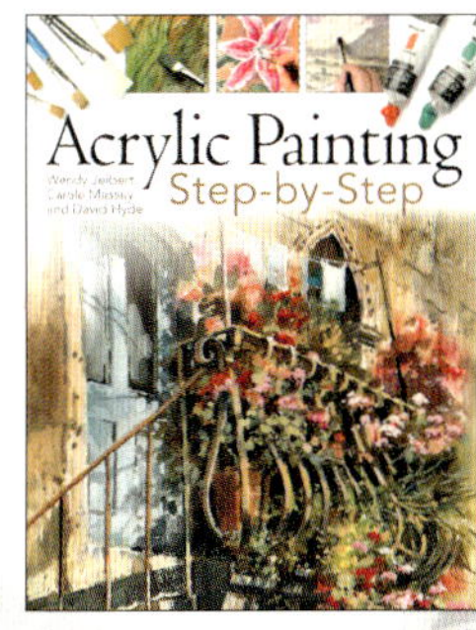

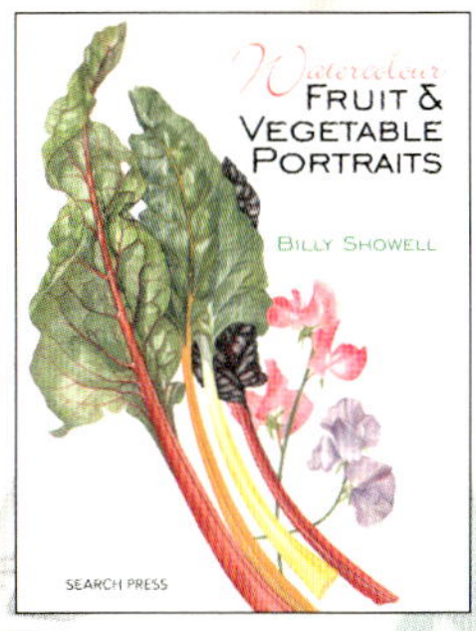

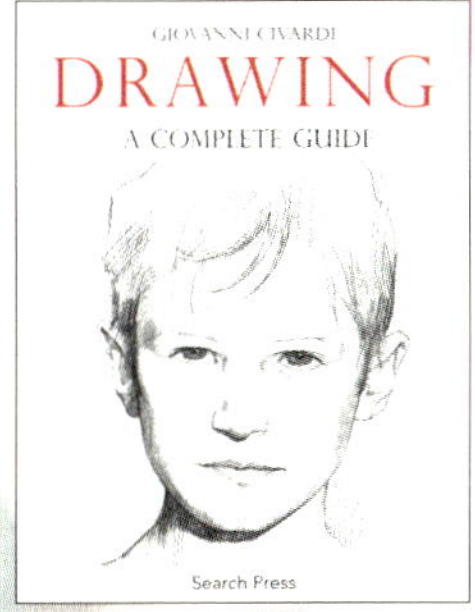

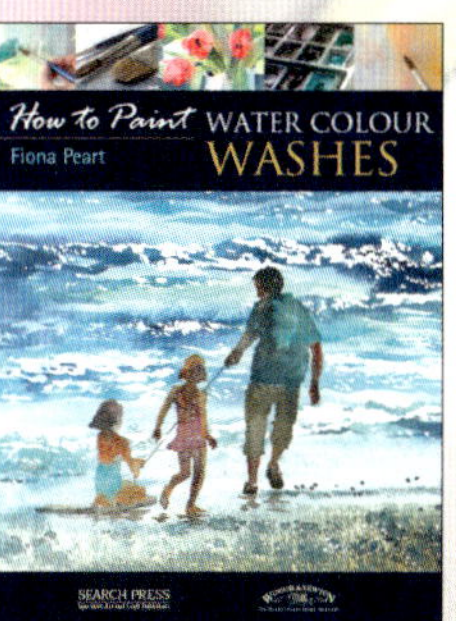

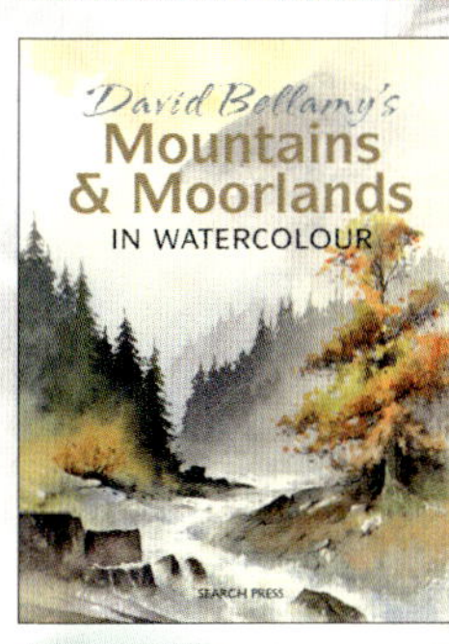

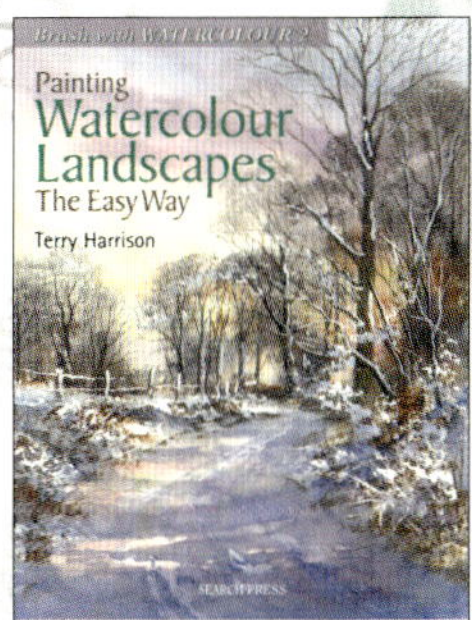

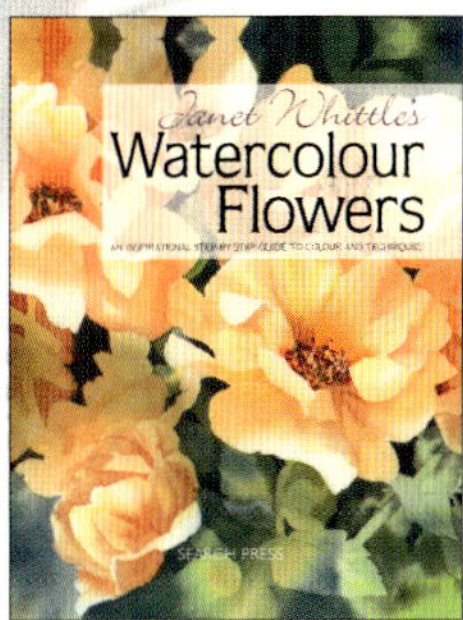

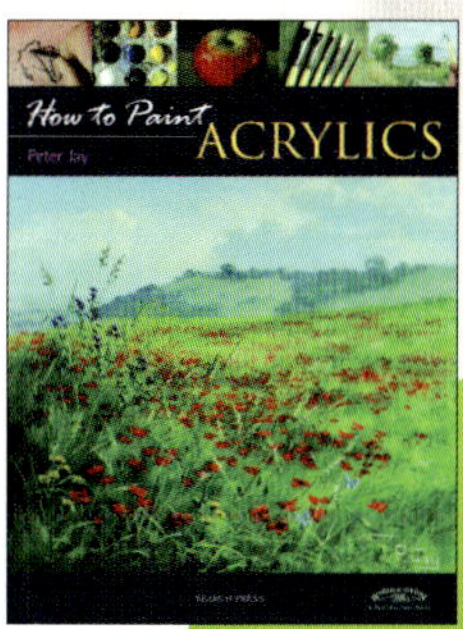

FOLLOW US ON:

twitter

www.twitter.com/searchpress

facebook

Search Press Art and Craft Books

To request a free catalogue, go to http://www.searchpress.com/requestcat.asp

People who want to learn to paint without relying on their drawing skills have everything they need in this book. Full of mood and atmosphere, the five beautiful coastal landscape paintings vary from a tranquil saltmarsh scene to the fresh aftermath of a storm. Tony Cowlishaw's detailed explanations are accompanied by step-by-step photographs.

- **6** pull-out, reusable tracings
- Over **200** step-by-step photographs
- Clear, practical advice

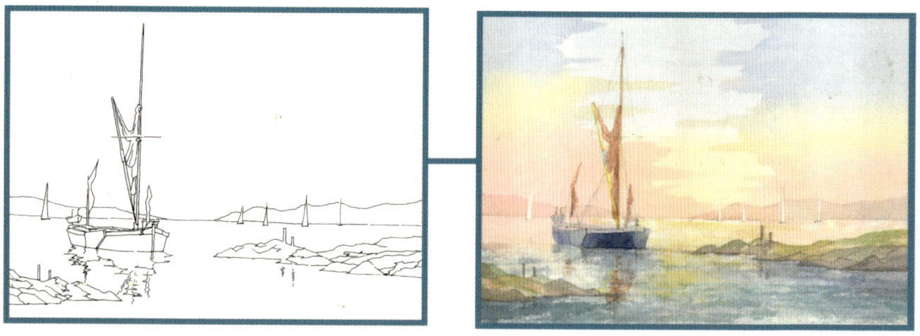

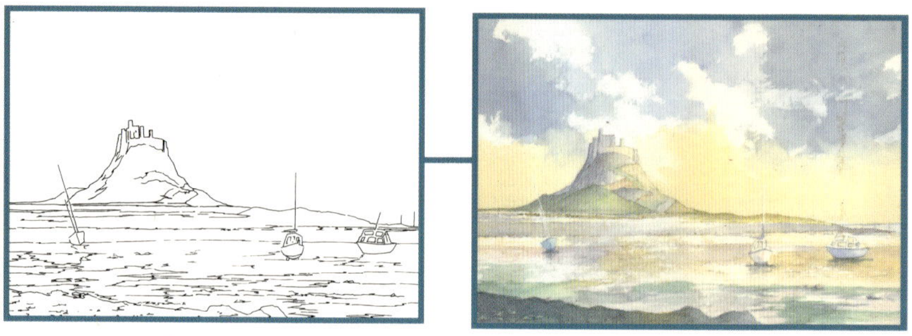

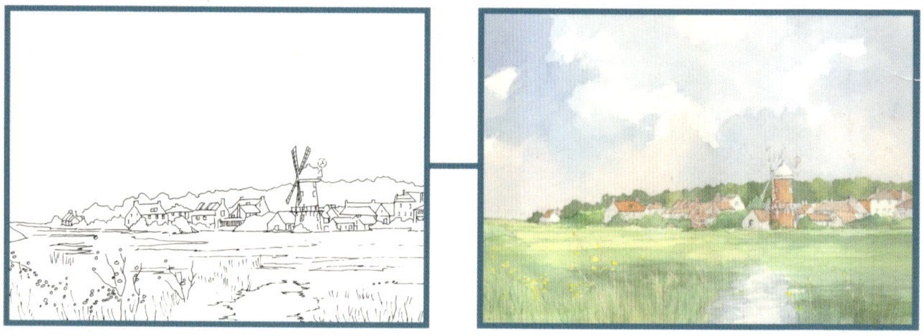

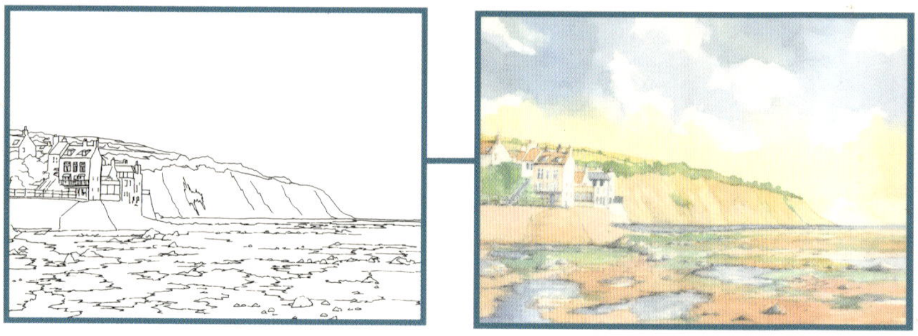

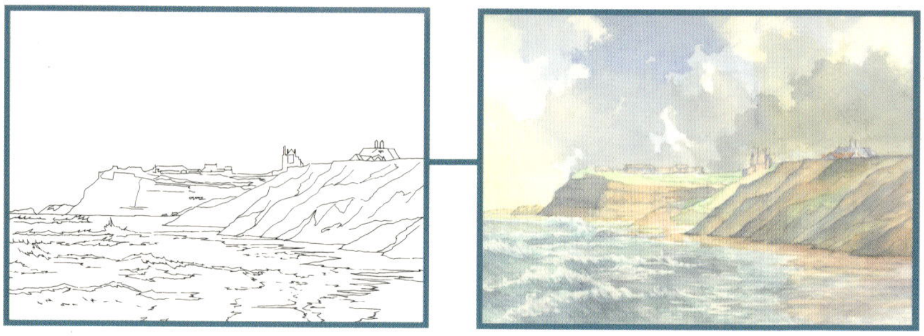

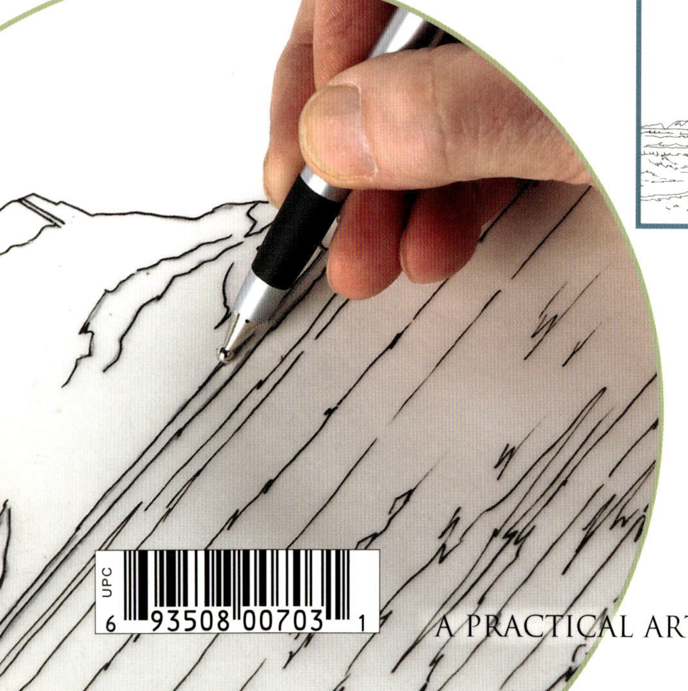

A PRACTICAL ART BOOK FROM SEARCH PRESS

Recommended retail price
UK £8.99 US $17.95
ISBN 978-1-84448-656-4
EAN
9 781844 486564 >
www.searchpress.com